THE SUNDERLAND FLYING-BOAT QUEEN

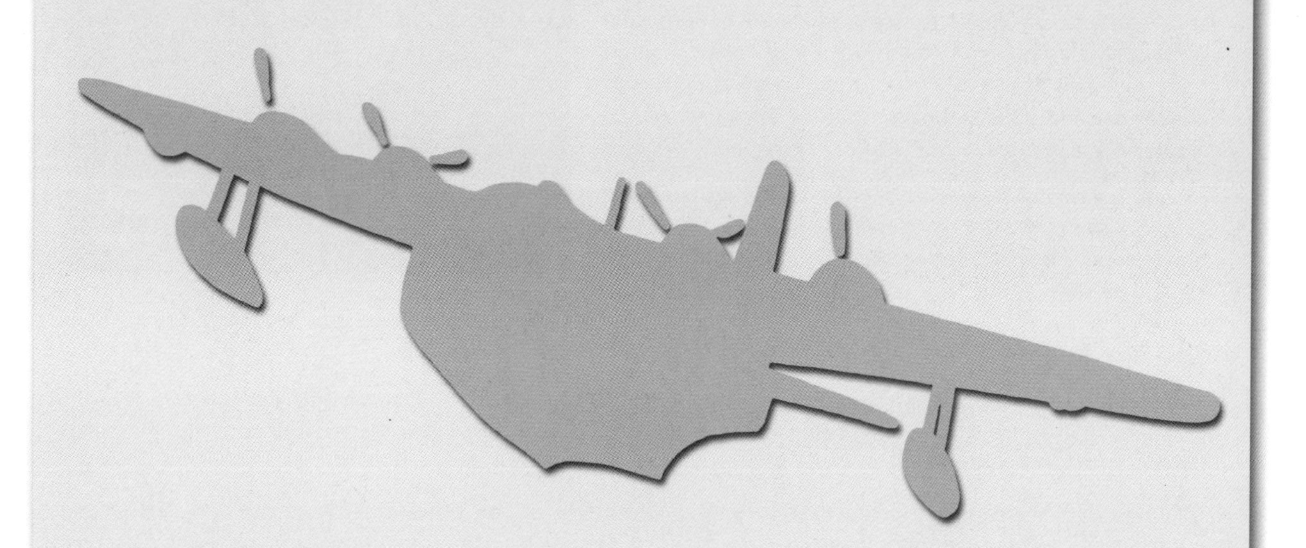

VOLUME III

John Evans.

JOHN EVANS

Foreword

My introduction to the world of the Webfooted Club was after my Cadet Course in the Royal Australian Air Force at Point Cook in 1939. A short course on Seagull (Walrus) amphibians preceded departure to the UK to join No 10 Squadron, RAAF, then forming at Pembroke Dock with Sunderlands.

First came a course at Calshot on Singapore IIIs before serving for two years, 173 operations and 1,996 flying hours, on the squadron.

During this period our Sunderlands were involved in a wide variety of tasks including convoy protection, anti-submarine and anti-shipping patrols, air-sea rescue, transporting war supplies to Egypt, shadowing and attacking enemy shipping, flying politicians, picking up German prisoners in the Bay of Biscay and landing at night to contact Allied troops trapped on Crete after the evacuation. There were others in which I was involved.

The Sunderland was a solid old beast which took a lot of punishment - both from ourselves and the enemy and thereby gained the respect of both. It was a self-contained unit having bunks, galley, toilet, workbench aft and a ship's clock and lockable cash box in the 'officer's wardroom'. Despite its peashooter .303 guns it gave a good account of itself against the 20mm guns of the Luftwaffe and the 20 and 40mm of the U-Boats and enemy merchant vessels.

Vic Hodgkinson when a BOAC Captain on the flying-boat fleet.

On return to Australia after my operational tour an immediate Catalina course awaited me and then I went to 20 Squadron, RAAF, in North Australia for another 44 operations against the Japanese in the North New Guinea and Solomon Islands areas. This increased my total hours to 3,000 and I commanded the squadron.

Next came a posting as chief flying instructor on Catalina and Walrus before returning to Sunderlands to form and command 40 Squadron, RAAF, for over a year at Port Moresby, New Guinea. These 'boats were stripped of armaments and used as transports in the New Guinea and North Australian theatre.

A staff course followed and shortly after I resigned my Commission as Wing Commander, with a total of 4,300 hours, to join British Overseas Airways Corporation in the UK. I flew their Sunderland civil conversions - the Hythe, Sandringham and Solent - on the Johannesburg, Sydney and Hong Kong/Japan services, bringing my total 'boat time to around 7,400 hours.

From 1950 - the end of BOAC flying-boat operations - to retirement in 1971 it was a different life on Argonaut, Britannia 102, Comet 4 and both Boeing 707-436 and –336 aircraft on worldwide services, totalling up a final figure of 19,320 flying hours.

Although all of these aircraft were a delight to operate my days on the 'boats were by far the best. They were a greater challenge and a more 'hands on' aircraft than these latter day semi-automatic flying machines. The Sunderland was among the best of the 'boats.

Over the years I have been actively involved in the restoration and maintenance of Sandringham 'Beachcomber' which is on display at the Southampton Hall of Aviation - now renamed 'Solent Sky'.

Gone are the days of pure salt air to be replaced by the smell of burning rubber! They call this progress?!

VIC HODGKINSON

Ex-Wing Commander, DFC, MID
Ex-Captain, BOAC
Master Air Pilot, Certificate 492
Service numbers: 2665 (as airman on joining up, 1937)
463 (on being commissioned)

Lymington
Hampshire

October 2004

Introduction

This is the long promised follow-up to my two earlier volumes on the Short Sunderland and reflects a lifetime's interest - some might say obsession - with an aircraft which will always remain one of the iconic types in British aviation history.

All three books between them reflect the many and varied roles of a truly remarkable and long serving aircraft and its service with many nations.

Once again, the majority of the photographs included have never been published before, coming from private collections and albums generously loaned to me over the years.

My all-abiding interest in flying-boats - and especially the Sunderland - has brought me into contact with so many who had special connections with the 'Queen of the flying-boats'. It has been a privilege to correspond with them and in many cases to meet up and chat with them, often at the memorable sequence of Flying-Boat Reunions staged at Pembroke Dock in the 1980s and 1990s.

I hope that they, particularly, will look upon this volume - and the earlier volumes which are still in print - as a worthy tribute to that most versatile and beautiful aircraft, the Short Sunderland.

John Evans

Pembroke Dock
October 2004

Camouflage... Up to the middle of the Second World War the Sunderlands carried 'all over' camouflage patterns. This was superceded by the predominantly white hulled appearance which is synonymous with the type through much of its long and meritorious service. This brand new Mark III, with full camouflage, performs for the Short Brothers cameraman, the picture dated July 3rd 1942. The lovely lines of the Sunderland are captured superbly.
SHORT BROS LTD via GREG WEBB

Yangtse... Against the stunning backdrop of Lion Rock Peak, 88 Squadron's D-Dog awaits the next call to duty at Kai Tak, Hong Kong. This is ML772, the famous 'Yangtse Sunderland' which in April 21st 1949 landed alongside the Royal Navy destroyer *HMS Amethyst* trapped on the Yangtse River by Chinese Communists. ML772's cameo role in the unfolding drama was later played out for the silver screen in the film 'Yangtse Incident'. The full story of the 'Yangtse Sunderland' is told in *Flying-Boat Queen* Volume I.
PAT UNSWORTH

Dedication

Dedicated to the memory of special friends among the flying-boat fraternity:

George Bunting, DFC (228 Squadron); Doug Kneale (228 Squadron); Jerry Morbey (88, 201, 228 and 230 Squadrons; Bill Millar (210 Squadron); Albert Taylor (210 Squadron) and Fred Weaver, AFC (88, 201, 205 and 230 Squadrons).

Chapter I Top Marks

Star of the show... The start of the Second World War was just weeks away when the Empire Air Day at Martlesham Heath was staged on May 20th 1939. A star of the show at the Suffolk airfield was the prototype Sunderland, K4774. Flying low over the airfield - home of the Aeroplane and Armament Experimental Establishment (A&AEE) - its sleek silver lines contrasted with biplane Gloster Gladiator fighters still in RAF service. First flown in October, 1937, K4774 was Number One out of 749 Sunderlands and derivatives - from Mark Is to Mark Vs - which served with distinction for the next 30 years. K4774 earned its keep in the war years carrying out many tests and trials at the Marine Aircraft Experimental Establishment's wartime home at Helensburgh. Surviving various mishaps, it was still flying in April 1944.
ALEX CARRIE

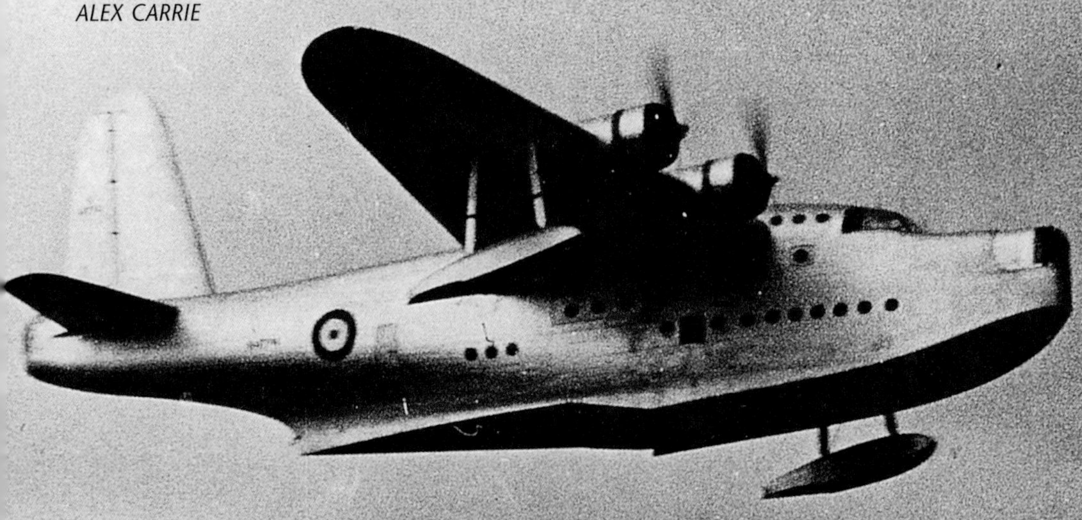

R.A.F.'S NEW 20-TON FLYING BOATS

RANGE OF 2,500 MILES

By Group Capt. L. G. S. Payne

Official details have now been released of the performance of the big, four-engine, 20-ton Short Sunderland flying boats, which are the standard equipment of several R.A.F. general reconnaissance squadrons. They were seen in flight over many Air Force aerodrimes on Empire Air Day.

These boats are armed with seven machine guns and powered by four Bristol Pegasus XXII. 1,010 h.p. engines. Their normal cruising speed is 178 m.p.h., they can reach a maximum speed of 210 m.p.h., and their extreme range is 2,500 miles.

Carrying full military load and equipment, the Sunderland can attain a height of 15,000ft. It has a wing area of 1,504 square feet, and can take off from the water in the remarkably short time of 33 seconds.

It's official... By June 1939 official information was being released about 'The RAF's new 20 ton flying-boats'. This is a report from the *Daily Telegraph* and *Morning Post*.
AUTHOR'S COLLECTION

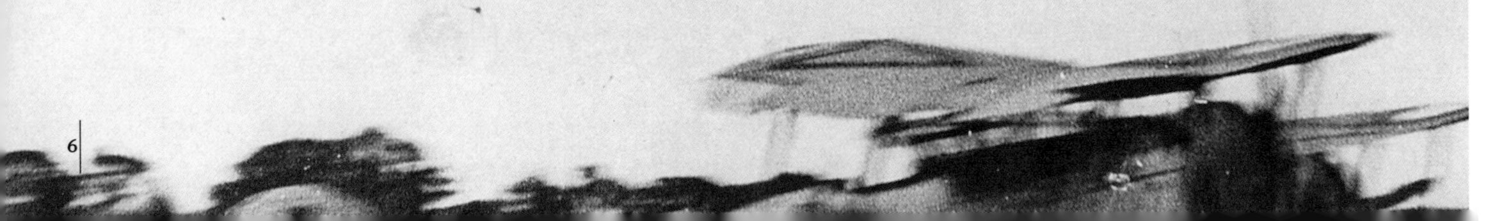

Factory fresh... Ashore for inspection at Calshot is brand new Mark I N9048. Accepted from the Shorts factory on September 11th 1939 it was soon in the hands of its rightful owners, the Royal Australian Air Force. The first of ten Sunderlands ordered by the Dominion for the newly formed No 10 Squadron, RAAF, all were scheduled to be flown to Australia, but the war changed that. Instead 10 Squadron became an integral part of RAF Coastal Command. N9048 - soon to carry the code combination, RB-A - carried out the first squadron operational flight, from Pembroke Dock to Stranraer, on 5th December with F/Lt Bill Garing in command. For the next 12 months N9048 flew long and hard. Its end came on the night of November 27th/28th 1940 during a Luftwaffe raid on Plymouth. The Mount Batten hangar containing N9048 received a direct hit and the aircraft was completely destroyed.
WING COMMANDER STAN BAGGOTT COLLECTION

Beaching... Unsung heroes in the complicated operation to beach a Sunderland were the two airmen who, complete with waterproof gear, had to brave varying water temperatures to assist. Here the front beaching legs and the tail trolley have been fitted to Mark I N9028 of 204 Squadron and the towing hawser attached. Launching a Sunderland was an equally skilful operation. N9028 had a short war with 204 Squadron - it was shot down by Luftwaffe fighters over Trondheim, Norway, on July 21st, 1940. All 12 crewmen - including 204's CO, W/Cdr E. S. C. Davis - were killed and are remembered on the Runnymede Memorial.
JOHN WITCOMB

Radar... A key part of the Sunderland's armoury as the war progressed was ASV (air to surface vessel) radar. The clean lines of the aircraft sprouted various aerials, on top and on the sides of the fuselage, under the wingtips and above the cockpit. W3993 of 10 Squadron, seen at Mount Batten, was an 'aerial festooned' Mark II. Rochester-built, W3993 had a successful sub-hunting career. On June 11th 1942 F/Lt Eric Martin and crew roughed up U-105 which was forced to put into a Spanish port. Nearly a year later - on 7th May 1943 and captained by F/Lt Geoff Rossiter who had been Martin's second pilot - W3993 made another sighting. This time there was no reprieve for the submarine and U-465, crippled in two separate attacks, later sank. W3993 lasted nearly two years with 10 Squadron. It was struck by another Sunderland at Mount Batten in October 1943 and although flown to Belfast was found to be beyond economic repair and written off.
BILL STARK/ALLAN STARK

Gunner... Mark I Sunderlands were fitted with twin midship gun positions, complete with single Vickers machine guns. A determined looking Steve Challen is pictured at his gun position on P9606 of 201 Squadron in September 1940. Steve - who later remustered as a pilot - is wearing a leather flying jacket, helmet and goggles; very necessary equipment for such an exposed position.
STEVE CHALLEN

Down the slip... EK575, its outer engines already running, takes to the waters at Pembroke Dock. This was a Blackburn-built Mark III, the most noticeable difference from earlier marks being the fully faired 'step' on the hull, giving the Sunderland's keel a much smoother line. Joining its first frontline unit, 461 Squadron, in August 1943, EK575 flew 33 operational trips before adopting something of a nomadic existence in 1944. Brief service with 228 Squadron was followed by spells with 423 RCAF and 10 RAAF Squadrons before being withdrawn from service in the November. A year later, with the war over, this was one of many Mark IIIs to be struck off charge.
MAP

Tall tails... The massive tailfin of Sunderland EK575 towers over Australian pilot Merv Pike at Pembroke Dock. He was guide to an official photographer who focused on this particular Mark III from a very unusual angle and a large version of the photo was later displayed in Australia House, London. Merv served twice with 461 Squadron at PD, initially as a first pilot and then with his own crew.
MERV PIKE

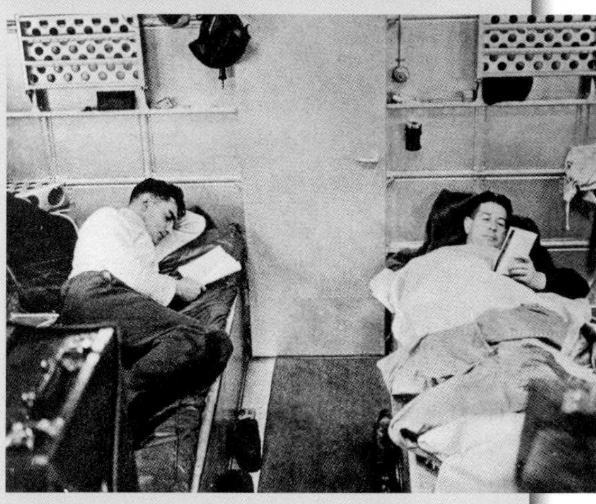

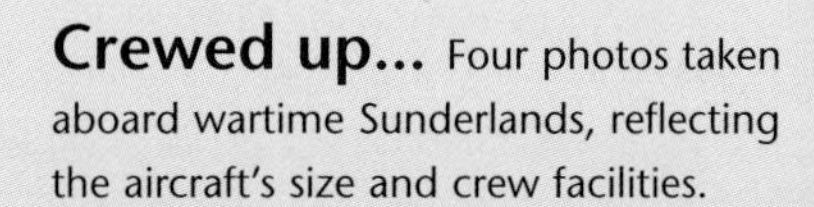

Crewed up... Four photos taken aboard wartime Sunderlands, reflecting the aircraft's size and crew facilities.

Top: The Navigator's station usually occupied by F/Sgt Fred Capes of 228 Squadron. This may be on Mark III EJ139 in which Fred Capes and his crew - skippered by F/O H. J. H. Debnam - failed to return from the Bay of Biscay on May 24th 1943. They were shot down by the heavily armed U-441.
TERRY CAPES

Second: Wireless Operator F/Sgt Ken Field, of 461 Squadron, in his radio compartment.
SQUADRON LEADER KEN FIELD

Third: Eggs sunny side up! The all-important task of cooking a hot meal in the galley, using the twin stoves. A tin of 'State Fair' is warming up!
GROUP CAPTAIN TOM HARVEY

Bottom: The wardroom was equipped with two bunks with ample room to stretch out. The books are, of course, aircraft manuals!
GROUP CAPTAIN TOM HARVEY

Seaford... The familiar lines of the Sunderland can still be traced but the Mark IV Sunderland became a radically different aeroplane with a new name - Seaford. First flown in August 1944 powered by 1,700 hp Bristol Hercules radials, the Mark IV was later modified with a larger fin and rudder and dorsal fillet. Two prototypes and just eight Seafords were built, all the production aircraft begin converted into civilian Solents. NJ205 served briefly on trials with 201 Squadron and later became G-AKNS, City of Liverpool, with national airline BOAC. It was briefly remustered for RAF service in November 1950, taking on new serial WM759 and undertaking trials with MAEE at Felixstowe, and was scrapped four years later.
MAP

Salute... A 'Queen of the Air' salutes a 'Queen of the Sea' - Sunderland Mk V SZ582 over the *Queen Elizabeth*. Bill Bailey and his 230 Squadron crew found themselves starring in this *Picture Post* photograph taken in 1947 or 1948. Like many others of his 'union', Navigator Harry Hopper was tasked with finding the royal liner on one of its Atlantic crossings. Built at Short and Harland, Belfast, SZ582 served only with 230 Squadron at Calshot between July 1947 and November 1948. It was then returned to Shorts and may have survived in storage until as late as 1957. Mark Vs were powered by American Pratt and Whitney Twin Wasps - the adoption of new engines extending the Sunderlands' operational life by over 20 years.
BILL BAILEY

Chapter II Calm Before The Storm

Stuka victim... Its silver hull already showing the scars of the sea, the fourth production Mark I, L2161, rests at a mooring, probably at Rochester. First flown on May 23rd 1938, L2161 was destined for Singapore arriving at Seletar two months later as part of the re-equipment of No 230 Squadron. In separate ceremonies four 230 Sunderlands were christened by the Sultans of the Federated Malay States which had funded the purchase of the aircraft. In November this Sunderland was christened 'Negri Sembilan'. L2161 moved with 230 to the Mediterranean in May 1940 where its adversaries were, initially, the Italians and then the Germans too. Nearly a year later - on April 23rd 1941 - L2161 was attacked when moored at Scaramanga, Greece, by several Junkers Ju87 dive bombers. The Stukas left the Sunderland ablaze but only after two of its gunners had put up a spirited defence which earned them gallantry medals.
FLIGHT REF 158678 via GREG WEBB

Haven tragedy... The shattered remains of the fuselage of L2162 of 210 Squadron following its crash in the Milford Haven Waterway on the night of September 20th 1938. This was the first Sunderland to be lost in RAF service, the crash coming as a sharp reminder of the hazards of operating flying-boats. After making several landings and take offs in Angle Bay L2162 crashed, turned over and broke its back. Two airmen were killed and others in the crew injured. The captain had been instructing two young pilots in night landings.
JOHN McILWRAITH

Floating Dock... Under stormy skies and against a wintery backdrop another of the first batch of production Sunderlands, L2165, undergoes trials on the RAF's Floating Dock. This is believed to be at Invergordon early in 1939. L2165 made the first operational patrol of the war with 210 Squadron - on September 3rd 1939 - and just 15 days later it was lost with all its crew in a crash in Milford Haven. F/Lt Ivor Davies and several of his crew are buried in Llanion Cemetery, Pembroke Dock.
DENNIS TEAGUE COLLECTION via DARELL JAGO

On show...
Alongside a Short Singapore III, a biplane forebear, Mark I L5804 undergoes engine checks outside one of RAF Pembroke Dock's massive hangars. Briefly on 210 Squadron's books, L5804 soon headed south to 230 Squadron at Seletar, and went on to see extensive war service.
(See Chapter III)
210 SQUADRON ARCHIVES / DICK MacCALLUM

Spirited... No 228 Squadron was the third unit to re-equip with Sunderlands, L5806 arriving at Pembroke Dock to join the squadron on December 9th 1938. After a brief period with the other PD unit, 210, this aircraft returned to the 228 fold just before the war began. In the Mediterranean the following year 228's Sunderlands laboured with many tasks in dangerous skies. On November 1st 1940 the squadron lost a Sunderland (N9020) to Italian fighters but the same fate did not befall L5806. Attacked by two Macchi MC200 monoplanes and a Fiat CR42 biplane near Malta, the Sunderland was extensively damaged and two crew injured. LAC Reg Barton led the spirited defence, remaining at his gun throughout the action and he was later awarded the DFM. His skipper, F/Lt Maurice 'Mo' Ware, received the DFC. Repaired, L5806 soldiered on, this time with 230 Squadron, but failed to return from patrol on 25th July 1942.
DICK MacCALLUM

Junkers attacks... Wearing a cloak of brown and green, N9046 stars in a Short Brothers advert. It was among the initial allocation to the fourth squadron to accept Sunderlands, No 204 at Mount Batten, joining the unit in July 1939. Months later - on April 3rd 1940 - N9046 survived repeated attacks from Junkers Ju88s in an running battle near a North Sea convoy. Initially attacked by two Junkers, a lull in the action was followed by the arrival of four more enemy which were driven off. The most sustained attacks came from no less than six Ju88s, one of which was sent crashing into the sea by deadly accurate fire from the Cpl Bill Lillie's tail turret. Another of the enemy was damaged and the pack then headed home, leaving F/Lt Frank Phillips and his crew to nurse their badly damaged aircraft back to Invergordon. Phillips was awarded the DFC and Lillie a well deserved DFM. N9046 became a total loss in October 1940 when it sank at Sullom Voe in the Shetlands after catching fire at moorings. On paper it lingered on, being struck off RAF charge in January 1941.
CHARLES FORD

Chapter III Battle Boats

The Battle of the Atlantic was one of the most important campaigns of World War II - and certainly the longest. From September 3rd 1939 until a month after VE-Day in 1945, Sunderlands were on patrol over the Atlantic wastes, deep into the Bay of Biscay and in northern latitudes. They also flew in the Mediterranean campaign. In all these areas the mighty flying-boats played a unique role on a big war stage, serving with various squadrons of many nationalities.

Pride... Two war machines which epitomised grace and power - the battlecruiser *HMS Hood*, pride of the Royal Navy, and the Sunderland, pride of RAF Coastal Command. This photograph, taken at Plymouth, shows one of first aircraft allocated to No 10 Squadron, RAAF, N9050, RB-D, with a lone crewman getting a grandstand view of the Navyís finest. N9050 had the dubious distinction of being the first 10 Squadron aircraft to encounter a Luftwaffe adversary - a Messerschmitt Me110 in July 1940. The encounter ended in a draw, both aircraft being damaged. After service with the Australians, N9050 joined 95 Squadron in West Africa and survived periods with 202 and, again, 95 Squadrons before taking up training duties at Alness. This veteran Mark I lasted until after D-Day, being struck off charge in July 1944.
JOHN H. EVANS

'Somewhere in England'...

A well known photograph used in various wartime publications, the story with it referring to Australian airmen with their flying-boats 'somewhere in England'. In fact, they were definitely in Wales - at RAF Pembroke Dock where 10 Squadron first formed up! Squadron CO W/Cdr Leon Lachal chats with four of the original pilots of No 10 - left to right, F/Lt Bill Gibson, F/Lt Charles Pearce, F/O Ivan Podger and F/Lt Bill Garing. In the first weeks of the war Pearce and Podger were among those who gained valuable experience by flying operationally with the RAF's 210 Squadron.
ROSEMARY HORRELL via PHIL TOMASELLI

Casualties... Within the space of a few weeks in 1943, at the height of the war against the U-Boat, all three of these 10 Squadron Sunderlands were lost.

Top: Mark III W4004/Z, seen taxiing, was shot down on May 17th while on an anti submarine patrol in the Bay of Biscay. F/Lt Keith McKenzie and his 11-man crew disappeared without trace.
P. H. T. GREEN COLLECTION

Middle: A second blow for the Australians came just three days later (May 20th) when W3986/U, one of the last of the Mark IIs, crashed on fire four miles from the Eddystone Lighthouse. F/Lt Denis Saunders and 11 crew had only taken off a few minutes earlier from Mount Batten; all were killed. W3986 had notched up two successful submarine attacks - damaging U-71 on June 5th 1942 and the Italian *Reginaldo Guiliano* on September 1st.
MAP

Bottom: Beached at St Mary's on the Isles of Scilly is RB-B, W4020. During an eventful 18 months on the squadron this aircraft tested out a new galley gun mounting which gave the Sunderland added fire power from the side. W4020's last flight, an anti submarine patrol off Cape Finisterre, was on August 1st 1943 with F/Lt Bob Fry in command. The crew spotted a U-Boat on the surface and immediately attacked. After a dummy run the Sunderland came in for a second attack and the U-Boat gunners quickly found their mark. Although badly hit Fry and crew pressed home the attack and accurately dropped the depth charges with dealt a mortal blow, the submarine sinking in perhaps half a minute. The crippled Sunderland attempted to ditch but plunged into the water. Naval escorts were quickly on the scene and rescued five crewmen clinging to one of the aircraft's floats while a sixth was plucked from the sea. Fry and five others were lost - adding to the ever lengthening roll of honour.
MRS MARJORIE WILLIAMS

Epic battle... Battered and broken, Mark III DD852/J is towed across Plymouth Harbour, its flying days with 10 Squadron well and truly over. DD852's final curtain came in September 1944 when, during a gale, a vessel dragged its anchor and collided with the flying-boat. Despite valiant efforts to save the Sunderland it was blown on to rocks in Jennycliffe Bay and subsequently wrecked during the salvage operation. A year earlier (on August 3rd 1943) in the Bay of Biscay DD852 had survived the attentions of no less than seven Junkers Ju88s in an hour-long air battle. Four members of the Sunderland crew received gallantry awards - DFCs for skipper F/O Alan Williams and navigator F/O Reg Gross and DFMs for Sgts Tony Owen and Bill Moser.
ANGUS MCVINISH

Battle crew... F/O Alan Williams and the crew of DD852 who thwarted the Junkers Ju88s in August 1943. Back row, left to right: Sgt Bart Simon, F/O Reg Gross, F/O Ray Berndt, F/O Alan Williams, F/O Alan Murray, F/Sgt Jim Guy and Sgt George Fry. Front row, left to right: Sgt Bill Moser, Sgt Angus McVinish, Sgt Tony Owen and F/Sgt Alan Bird. An RAF passenger, F/Lt Dormey, was also on board during the battle.
ANGUS McVINISH

Line astern... Sunderlands take second place in this line up to one of the large G-class flying-boats which were commandeered for RAF service early in the war. The three S26 G-boats - *Golden Fleece, Golden Hind* and *Golden Horn* - were called up in September 1940 to bolster the RAF's hard pressed Sunderlands and given RAF serials. Major engineering was required to convert them to their military role. Twin dorsal turrets were installed plus a four-gun tail turret, bomb racks and radar. The G-boats equipped G Flight at Bowmore on Loch Indaal, Islay - where the photo was probably taken - and this unit became 119 Squadron in February 1941. After a period without aircraft 119 finally received Sunderlands late in 1942 but disbanded the following April, its aircraft and crews being dispersed to other squadrons.
DR A. A. DUNCAN via DAVID SMITH

Big sister... Sporting turrets and a full array of ASV aerials, camouflaged G-class X8275 - the former G-AFCK, *Golden Hind* - looks very much a military machine at Pembroke Dock in October 1941. Weeks later the two remaining G-boats (X8274, *Golden Fleece* having been lost in June) were returned to civilian use and Sunderlands were later posted in to 119 Squadron.
TIM WILSON

This way... A group of 119 Squadron personnel (most appear to be ground staff) photographed at Pembroke Dock in September 1941, not long before the squadron became non-operational. At the time the CO was W/Cdr A. G. F. Stewart.
TIM WILSON

In the 'clan'... Sunderland W6014 S for Sugar provides the backdrop as the CO and senior aircrew of 201 Squadron line up for a formal photo at Lough Erne in late 1942 or early 1943. At the time the CO was W/Cdr J. B. Burnett. The Squadron had joined the Sunderland 'clan' in April 1940, having gone to war with obsolete London biplanes. This was the beginning of a long and meritous association between one of the RAF's oldest squadrons and the Sunderland, finally ending 17 years later. A Mark III, W6014 joined 201 in November 1942 and operated with the squadron for well over a year. It completed its service on the training circuit with 4 OTU and was struck off charge in July 1945.
GROUP CAPTAIN TOM HARVEY

Oceanus... In wartime few Sunderlands were given names, one of the exceptions being T9087, ZM-O, of 201 Squadron which was discreetly dubbed 'Oceanus'. T9087 joined 201 in February 1942 and survived well over a year of active service before being transferred to Scottish Aviation in July 1943. It was struck off charge the following February.
CHRIS ASHWORTH COLLECTION

At Lough Erne... The crew of ZM-O perched around the name Oceanus at Lough Erne, Northern Ireland, in 1942.
WING COMMANDER DEREK MARTIN

Awards... Tents are the background for this shot of 201 Squadron skipper F/Lt Eddie Bent and crew members. Joining them are F/Lt Ivor Wiles, an Australian member of the squadron, and F/Lt Les Baveystock who, in 1944, was awarded a Bar to his DFC and a DSO for successful attacks on U-Boats. Baveystock inherited Bent's crew after the skipper became tour expired. Pictured are (all left to right) back row: Sgt Cottrell, Sgt Parsons, ? , Sgt Macree, Sgt Bullock. Middle: F/Lt Ivor Wiles, P/O Ian Riddell, F/Lt Eddie 'Badly' Bent, F/O Brian Landers, F/Lt Les Baveystock. Front: Sgt Howarth, F/Sgt Paton, F/Sgt Perrin.
BRIAN LANDERS/ IVOR WILES

Launching... Outer engines already running, Mark I N9021 is prepared for launching at RAF Mount Batten. It carries the KG-G codes of 204 Squadron, then resident at the Plymouth station. The squadron received Sunderlands before the war began and was soon on the move, firstly to the Shetlands for patrols off Norway and over the important U-Boat and German surface raider transit area of the Denmark Strait. A further move came in April 1941 to Reykjavik, Iceland, but within weeks 204 was heading for the warmer climes of West Africa. N9021 was transferred to 201 Squadron in October 1940 and was lost before the year's end. Returning from a convoy escort on December 15th the crew was diverted to Invergordon. A float was damaged and the aircraft turned turtle and sank, thankfully after all the crew had been taken off.
WING COMMANDER VIC HODGKINSON

At Gib... The dramatic outline of Gibraltar's famous Rock serves to identify the location for Mark I L5798 of 204 Squadron. For a long time DA-A of 210 Squadron, L5798 survived five intense years of operational flying with 210, 201 and 204 Squadrons. The weather rather than the enemy finally put paid to this venerable lady's career. Damaged in a gale at Gibraltar in September 1943, L5798 was flown back to Calshot but was found to be beyond economic repair, and scrapped.
Via CHAZ BOWYER

Record breaker... To No 210 Squadron at Pembroke Dock went the distinction of pioneering the Sunderland into RAF service. L2159, the second production one, was first flown to PD on May 20th 1938 and a few days later was the undoubted star of the station's annual Empire Air Day. Its time with 210 was brief as L2159 was part of the re-equipment of 230 Squadron at Singapore. On June 9th F/Lt W. A. Hughes and crew took L2159 from Milford Haven at the start of a record flight to Seletar, arriving on June 22nd. Their route was Gibraltar, Malta, Alexandria, Lake Habbaniya, Bahrein, Karachi, Gwalior, Calcutta, Dala River, Rangoon, Mergui, Seletar. Only minor hiccup en route was a forcelanding at Dala River, at the mouth of the Irrawaddy, due to monsoon conditions. Although posted east, L2159 ended up a war casualty back in the UK. While moored at Greenock, Scotland, in May 1941 this record-breaking Sunderland was destroyed in a Luftwaffe raid.
DAVE ROWE

Mystery... From its DA codes this is a 210 Squadron aircraft but its actual identity has not been determined. However it may by N9026, a Mark I which joined the squadron at Pembroke Dock in May 1939. In one of the mysteries of the maritime war N9026 and its crew simply disappeared without trace from a patrol on June 29th 1940. There was one clue - Dutch airmen recently arrived at Pembroke Dock listened in to German radio and heard a claim that a four-engined aircraft had been shot down that day. This could only have been a Sunderland. South African Allan Ainslie, a very experienced skipper, and the other eight members of N9026's crew are commemorated on the Runnymede Memorial.
WARREN SUTTON

Bombing up... Day-by-day tasks for Sunderland groundcrew included the very physical effort of bombing up aircraft ready for the next operation. Here three airmen work on N9022 of 210 Squadron, probably at Pembroke Dock before the move to Oban in July 1940. The 250 lb anti-submarine bombs with which the Sunderlands were first equipped proved ineffective against the U-Boat. It was only with the adoption of the naval depth charge, modified for dropping from the air, that Coastal Command really got some 'teeth' to use against submarines. N9022 was a Mark I which joined 210 Squadron in March 1939, spending some time with 204 Squadron before returning to 210. On December 27th 1940 N9022 crashed at Oban with the loss of F/Lt Ivor Meggitt and nine crew. There was one survivor, F/O D. A. Stewart.
ROCKY STONE

Officers... No 228 Squadron's CO, W/Cdr Gilbert Nicholetts, pictured with his officer aircrew in May 1940 - a rare moment when so many were together at Pembroke Dock. Nicholetts had a long connection with flying-boats and was one of the original pilots with the Far East Flight at Seletar, Singapore, in 1927/28. He was a PoW of the Japanese for three years and retired from the post-war RAF as Air Marshal Sir Gilbert. Pictured are (all left to right), Back row: P/O Gooch, P/O Trotter, P/O Rushton, P/O Stewart, F/O Laurie Ellis, P/O Lawrence Jones, DFC, F/O Farries, F/O Pyne, P/O Frank Goyen and P/O Mason. Front row: P/O Trippe, F/O David Bevan John, F/Lt David McKinley, DFC, F/Lt Thurston Smith, DFC, S/Ldr Guy Menzies, W/Cdr Nicholetts, AFC, F/Lt John Brooks, F/Lt Burnett, F/Lt Maurice Ware and F/Lt Robert Craven, DFC.
WING COMMANDER LAURIE ELLIS, DFC/
WING COMMANDER MAURICE WARE, DFC

Aground... Unexpected arrival at Invergordon on April 28th 1940 was 228 Squadron Sunderland N9025, aground but undamaged. Carrying the code combination DQ-Y, N9025 had just returned from Norway and events which earned its captain and first pilot a DFC each. With the German invasion in full swing, F/Lt Bobby Craven and crew had been tasked to take British personnel to Andalsnes and landed in Molde Fjord near to *HMS Witherington*. With Luftwaffe attacks continuing Craven and his passengers went aboard the destroyer leaving P/O Lawrence 'Slim' Jones in charge. The waterborne Sunderland attracted further Luftwaffe attention so Jones took off, only to be attacked by a Messerschmitt Me110 fighter when at 150 feet. Accurate return fire from the Sunderland so damaged the German that it crashed inland. Jones landed to pick up his skipper and the crew returned home the following day. N9025 was undamaged from its grounding and within weeks was dispatched to the Mediterranean with F/Lt Thurston Smith and crew. There on August 6th it was shot down by Italian fighters and most of the crew made prisoners of war.
AIR MARSHAL SIR ROBERT CRAVEN, DFC

Press report... How the DFC awards to Craven and Jones were announced in the national press. F/Lt Craven went on to Air Rank in the RAF, retiring as Air Marshal Sir Robert.
228 SQUADRON ARCHIVES

GALLANTRY IN THE AIR

AWARDS APPROVED BY THE KING

SKILL IN FIGHTING

The King has been pleased to approve the following awards in recognition of gallantry displayed in flying operations against the enemy:—

DISTINGUISHED FLYING CROSS

CRAVEN, Acting Flight Lieutenant Robert Edward.
This officer was captain and pilot of a flying-boat which proceeded on a special journey to Norway in very bad weather in April. On arrival at his destination he handled his aircraft with great skill and gallantry and disembarked his passengers in the face of persistent enemy bombing attacks. The return journey was successfully accomplished on the following day in spite of adverse weather conditions. Flight Lieutenant Craven displayed great determination, courage, and perseverance in carrying out this hazardous mission.

JONES, Pilot Officer Lawrence Latham.
This officer was second pilot and navigator of a flying-boat engaged on a special journey to Norway in April. During the temporary absence of his captain, after a landing had been made, Pilot Officer Jones assumed command and successfully manoeuvred his aircraft on the water to avoid the intense bombing attacks by enemy aircraft. Subsequently it became necessary to take off, but he was attacked by an enemy fighter shortly afterwards. By skilful tactics he brought his tail guns to bear and the enemy was shot down. This officer showed skill and gallantry of a very high order.

Malta... The beleaguered island of Malta and the Mediterranean area were very familiar to 228 Squadron during the early years of the war. Kalafrana, the flying-boat station on Malta, was home base for a time and the picture shows Sunderland DQ-R of 228 under tow there. This may well be L5807 which was strafed and sunk at its Kalafrana mooring on April 27th 1941.
PHIL VERNON

Purple Patch... For the last two years of the war 228 Squadron was based back at RAF Pembroke Dock, where it had formed up as a flying-boat unit in 1936. During this period it notched up several attacks on U-Boats and was credited with sinking five. There was a purple patch of successful attacks in 1943. On May 31st F/O Bill French and crew in DD838 provided the coup de gras on U-563, sharing the kill with a 10 Squadron Sunderland DV969 (F/Lt Max Mainprize) and a RAF Halifax. On July 13th F/O Reader Hanbury successfully dispatched U-607, and he followed this up on August 2nd with an attack on U-106, sharing the success with DV968 of 461 Squadron (F/Lt I. A. F. Clarke). 'Hank' Hanbury was flying JM708 on both occasions. The day before Hanbury's second attack F/Lt Stan White in JM678 sank U-383. The fifth confirmed kill came just after D-Day when F/Lt Gordon Lancaster in ML877 sank U-970 on June 7th 1944. Hanbury was awarded the squadron's only wartime DSO and there were DFCs for the other pilots. In the last months of the war 228 became the only RAF squadron to be fully equipped with the new Mark V Sunderlands. Final operational roles for the 228 aircrews were to shepherd surrendering U-Boats into Royal Navy hands. Among the Mark Vs flown on these patrols was PP118, UE-P, seen below. Later serving with 201 and 230 Squadrons, PP118 joined 235 Operational Conversion Unit at Calshot. It sank at moorings in February 3rd 1950, was salvaged but then caught fire and burnt out on February 23rd. *GROUP CAPTAIN J. W. LOUW COLLECTION*

Sub double... A hazy photo depicting the end of one of the most successful of submarine hunting Sunderlands. This was L5804 of 230 Squadron which on successive days in June 1940 dealt a double blow to the Italian Navy, not long after Italy had entered the war on the Axis side. Piloted by F/Lt William Campbell, L5804 attacked and sank the *Argonauta* on the 28th and the next day repeated the feat over the *Rubino*, landing nearby to rescue four survivors. Campbell was awarded the DFC. A month later L5804 - captained by S/Ldr Ryley - survived an hour-long battle with three Italian Macchi MC200 fighters off Sicily, returning to Malta in a badly holed aircraft and three wounded gunners. L5804 fought on in the maelstrom of the Mediterranean war. As the disastrous Greek campaign developed 230's hard pressed Sunderlands were detailed with more tasks, a detachment operating from Scaramanga, a Greek Navy base on Lake Eleusis, not far from Athens. It was here that L5804 sank at its moorings in a gale on February 25th 1941. The aircraft appears to have been salvaged but was unserviceable and left behind when the Germans invaded Greece. Rumours circulated later that the Germans had flown a Sunderland and L5804 seemed a likely candidate. However, no documentary evidence has come to light to support these stories.
MIKE TAYLOR

Evacuation... Behind this seemingly peaceful scene lies a story of tenacity and heroism. Sunderlands of 230 and 228 Squadrons flew many sorties during the disastrous Greek campaign to rescue military and civilian personnel - including royalty - from the advancing enemy. NM-X of 230 is pictured from another Sunderland awaiting its next passengers. Following the invasion of Crete Sunderlands were cast in the same evacuation role. On one occasion no less than 82 people were wedged into a Sunderland.
IMPERIAL WAR MUSEUM

Boatmen... An Air Ministry photograph captioned 'A group of RAF flying-boat pilots who did such magnificent work in connection with the British withdrawl from Greece'. Among the boatmen are 230 Squadron pilots, far left, Lionel Powell; third from left, Odhams; seated front, Woodward; centre back, Alan Lywood; second from right, Brand.
WING COMMANDER ALAN LYWOOD

New colours... One of the handful of flying-boats which served so magnificently in the Greek and Crete evacuations was N9029 which had joined 230 Squadron as long ago as July 1939. By mid 1942 this well travelled aircraft was sporting new camouflage and new DX squadron codes, but retained the V for Victory individual letter. Still with 230 Squadron, N9029 was lost in a crash on New Year's Day 1943.
FRED MOCK

Beached... High and dry like a stranded whale, W6058 was none the worse for its unscheduled beaching in a Scottish gale. Belonging to the short-lived and little photographed 246 Squadron, this is probably the result of an incident at Loch Indaal in February 1943 when, as the port float filled with water, the aircraft was cast off from its mooring and came ashore. W6058 was one of the first batch of Sunderlands built at Short and Harland, Belfast. A late version Mark II, complete with top turret, W6058 went to No 330 Squadron and survived another incident - this time in the air - when the starboard outer propeller flew off during an operation trip from Sullom Voe. No 246 Squadron's time as a Sunderland unit was brief - reforming at Bowmore on September 1st 1942 and disbanding on April 30th the following year. It aircraft and crews were re-allocated to Nos 228, 330 and 422 Squadrons. W6058's career was equally brief. Joining 246 in October 1942 it passed to 330 Squadron and became a ground instructional airframe, number 4798M.
IMPERIAL WAR MUSEUM CH 10191

Of many nations... Among the men of many nationalities who flew Sunderlands were Norwegians of No 330 Squadron. For two years the squadron had operated from Iceland, flying Northrop single engined floatplanes. In early 1943 the squadron transferred to Oban and converted onto Sunderlands, flying Marks IIIs and Vs up to the end of the war. One of its Mark IIIs, NJ177, is pictured during maintenance ashore. Although this aircraft did not join 330 until July 1944 at least one of the Northrops was still around then and is pictured in the distance. NJ177 served with the squadron until the war was over. Converted to Mk V standard it did a stint with 209 Squadron in the Far East in 1953/54 and was damaged beyond repair in an accident in August 1954.
CATO GUHNFELDT COLLECTION

Parked... Neatly parked at RAF Killadeas, Northern Ireland, right at the end of the European war is this Mark V carrying the WH codes of 330 Squadron. Tantalisingly its RN serial number is covered by the efficient looking straps holding the aircraft down. It could well be RN267 which appears to be the only RN serial Sunderland to be allocated to 330. RAF Killadeas was the home of 131 OTU where Catalina and Sunderland crews were trained for wartime roles.
HARRY VERNON

'Fine Bombish'... Seconds away from touchdown at Castle Archdale is EK591 one of 422 Squadron's successful sub hunters. On March 10th 1944 W/O Frank Morton and his newly trained crew were joined for a patrol by experienced captain F/Lt Sid Butler. When a U-Boat was sighted Butler was flying and his attack proved fatal for U-625. The crippled submarine briefly submerged before resurfacing. For nearly 90 minutes the Sunderland plodded a circuit until suddenly the U-Boat flashed a signal 'Fine bombish' and its crew abandoned ship, leaving the vessel to slip stern first beneath the waves. For this action Butler was awarded the DFC and Morton was commissioned. Their aircraft, EK591, survived the war having spent a year at the Alness OTU and was stuck off charge in November 1945. No 422 Squadron was one of two Royal Canadian Air Force units to operate Sunderlands.
PUBLIC ARCHIVES OF CANADA PL40993
via CHAZ BOWYER

Upgraded... A busy Sunderland scene at Pembroke Dock includes ML874 carrying the DG-U codes of 422 Squadron. ML874 - designated a Mark IIIA as its upgraded radar scanners were now in neat under wingtip housings - also served with 270 Squadron before joining the French squadron, No 343. Upgraded to Mark V standard it kept its French connection with Aeronavale and was destroyed at Port Etienne in November 1948 when a supply launch exploded.
PUBLIC ARCHIVES OF CANADA PL41242
via CHAZ BOWYER

They also served... W/Cdr Jack Sumner, DFC, who commanded 422 Squadron from late 1944 until after the war ended, joined groundcrew for a formal photograph at Pembroke Dock. Without the dedication and skills of a devoted groundcrew no Sunderland squadron would have been able to function.
MRS DOROTHY LEWIS

Farewell... Their Coastal Command tasks completed the aircrew of 422 Squadron line up for a last photograph at Pembroke Dock in May 1945. The camouflaged hangar doors - so familiar a feature at PD - and a Mark III Sunderland are the backdrop.
422 SQUADRON ASSOCIATION via JACK LOGAN

First op... The first operation carried out by the new 423 Squadron, RCAF, was in Mark II W6053, AB-E - seen here at Oban in August 1942 - when F/Lt Musgrave and crew searched for a submarine in the Atlantic. From Oban 423 moved to Castle Archdale on Lough Erne and remained there for the rest of the war. Belfast built by Short and Harland, W6053 moved on to 330 Squadron in May 1943 and went into storage at Wig Bay a year later, being pensioned off finally at the war's end.
JIM WRIGHT

Double attack... A Boxing Day 1942 shot of members of Sunderland F for Freddie's crew, plus a couple of groundcrew, from 423 Squadron at Castle Archdale. F/O Howell and his crew went on to make a double attack on a U-Boat in March 1943 while second pilot F/O Al Bishop - by then in command of his own crew in Sunderland DD859 - sank U-489 in August 1943. Bishop's victim was a 'Milch Cow' - a large tanker-submarine used to re-supply other U-Boats. Caught on the surface south of Iceland the U-boat fought back and as Bishop made his level approach the Sunderland was repeatedly hit and crewmen injured. Bishop pressed home his attack and dropped six depth charges with deadly effect. Mortally damaged the Sunderland was ditched and cartwheeled into the sea with the loss of five of the crew. Bizarrely, Bishop and the survivors were soon joined by the U-Boat crew who abandoned ship close by, the submarine taking its last dive and exploding soon after. The Sunderlanders and the U-Boat survivors steadfastly ignored each other before rescue arrived from the Royal Navy. Bishop was awarded a well deserved DFC. In the picture are (all left to right), back row: Sgt G. Howard (WOM/AG); ACI J. Cross (flight mechanic airframes); Sgt M. W. Bird (WOp/AG); Sgt D. M. Proudlock (WOp/ AG); Cpl R. G. Lyster (flight mechanic airframes). Front row: Sgt C. J. Mason (engineer); Sgt C. B. Steeves (2nd navigator); F/O B. Howell (captain); F/O A. A. Bishop (1st pilot); P/O N. Martin (navigator).
CHARLIE MASON

Under tow... A tractor provides the horse power as EK593 is manoeuvred on the Castle Archdale slipway in July 1944. EK583 carries the figure 3 which was adopted for a time by 423 Squadron at the Northern Ireland base. Joining 423 in November 1943, this aircraft had just nine months of frontline service before transferring to training duties further along Lough Erne at Killadeas. Placed in store in May 1945, EK583 was scrapped in 1947.
Via ANDY THOMAS

Serial... A stern view of DP191, then a Mark III with 423 Squadron at Castle Archdale in November 1943, a month after joining the unit. Eight months later DP191 joined the Killadeas OTU and went into storage post war. Unlike most of its contemporaries DP191 dodged the scrapman and in 1953 was given a new lease of life - and a new serial NZ4109 - as a Mark V with the Royal New Zealand Air Force. Sadly, the scrapman finally caught up with this Windermere-built veteran in the mid 1960s.
JIM WRIGHT

Outward bound... Heading on an Atlantic patrol is DP200, one of 35 Sunderlands built on Lake Windermere where Short Brothers had established a wartime factory. At the time the figure 2 was used by 461 Squadron at Pembroke Dock. DP200 spent from March 1944 to January 1945 with 461, completing 40 operational trips, before returning to Shorts. The war ended before it returned to service. Converted to Mark V status DP200 came out of store in February 1954 to join 230 Squadron, also at Pembroke Dock. It was pensioned off in October 1956 as the home-based Sunderland squadrons began to run down and was sold for scrap in October 1957.
FRANK BAKER

Grandstand... One of Coastal Command's senior officers had a grandstand view of a U-Boat attack when flying with 461 Squadron. Air Vice-Marshal Brian Baker was aboard Sunderland JM676 on April 29th 1943 when a submarine was depth charged. F/O Raleigh Gipps, on his first operational trip as captain, attacked the surfaced U-Boat in spectacular fashion, as the photograph shows. The U-Boat was seen to sink and later the Admiralty assessed it as 'sunk'. In fact U-119, a 1,600 ton minelayer, had survived to continue its mission, only to be sunk by the Royal Navy two months later.
GROUP CAPTAIN A. M. CAREY

Numbers up... In an amazing coincidence Sunderland U of 461 dispatched submarine U-461 on July 30th 1943 - the 'kill' going to F/Lt Dudley Marrows and crew flying W6077. U-461 was one of three submarines transiting the Bay of Biscay in daylight, and prepared to fight their way through. Two were sunk by Coastal Command aircraft and the third was accounted for by Royal Navy escort vessels. Marrows and crew found themselves on the receiving end in mid September when they were attacked by six Junkers Ju88s off the Spanish coast. After a lengthy air battle Marrows ditched his battered Sunderland, EK578, and the crew was later rescued by *HMS Woodpecker*. The picture is of Marrows and crew after the July action and U-Boat sinking. Back row, all left to right: F/O Piers Taplin (2nd pilot); Sgt J. Jainer; F/O Jock Rolland (navigator); F/Lt Dudley Marrows (captain); F/O Jim Leigh (1st pilot); Sgt 'Bunny' Sydney (gunner); F/O Peter Jensen (WOp/AG). Front: Sgt Bert Webster (WOp/AG); Sgt Gerald 'Paddy' Watson (1st engineer); Sgt A. N. 'Bubbles' Pearce (2nd engineer, with dog); Sgt F. 'Pierre' Bamber and F/Sgt 'Horrie' Morgan.
GERALD WATSON

Gongs... Following a successful attack on U-270 on August 13th 1944 by Sunderland ML735 three members of its 461 Squadron crew received 'gongs'. Sporting their medal ribbons are, left to right: Captain, F/O Don Little, DFC, second pilot F/Sgt Fred Robinson, DFM, and navigator F/Lt Mac McInnes, DFC. In a night attack, Little and crew surprised the U-Boat on the surface, illuminated it with flares and straddled it with depth charges.
FRED ROBINSON

Crew shot... An occasion repeated by countless aircrews - the formal crew photo which in years to come would be a special reminder of wartime comradeship and friendships and of extraordinary and dangerous times. This is Don Goode's 461 Squadron crew taken at Pembroke Dock in 1945. Eight Australians and three RAF personnel make up the group. They are, all left to right, back row: P/O Jackie Auld (gunner); P/O R. D. Allan (pilot); P/O Johnny Hodge (gunner); F/Sgt Alec McCully (engineer); F/Sgt Bill Stenning (WOp/AG); F/Sgt Ken Hobson (WOp/AG). Front row: F/Sgt Vic Ferns (engineer); W/O Eric Muir (pilot); F/Lt Don Goode (captain); P/O Pat Howard (navigator) and F/Sgt Alfie Willy (WOM/AG). Don Goode and crew in NJ264 were involved in an air-sea rescue on April 27th 1945 after witnessing a Sunderland from 228 Squadron crash into the sea.
ALEC McCULLY

Chapter IV African Warriors

Vast expanses of the South Atlantic were patrolled by Sunderlands for four long years of war. Increased U-Boat activity against convoys making the long voyage around the South African Cape prompted the dispatch of Sunderlands to West Africa in 1941. Freetown, Bathurst, Jui, Dakar and many other places soon became very familiar names and territory to aircrews and the long suffering groundcrews who had to maintain the aircraft in harsh, uncompromising conditions and locations with the barest of facilities. From early 1941 until the war's end Sunderland squadrons operated over the South Atlantic in a war theatre largely overlooked on a world scale.

Destination Africa.... No 95 Squadron was formed in January 1941 from a flight of 210 Squadron - destination Africa! The squadron remained firmly African based until the end of the conflict, disbanding in June 1945. This squadron group was taken at RAF Jui early on in 95's long sojourn under African skies - either in 1941 or 1942.
CHARLES FORD

Mercy missions.... Moored against a dramatic background, Mark III JM671 is seen at St Vincente, Cape Verde Islands. This was part of 95 Squadron's 'beat' and regular 'mercy missions' were made there bringing serum to combat yellow fever. A Rochester-built Mark III, JM671 only served with 95 Squadron and did over two years in African skies. It was struck off charge in June 1945. In 1944/5 flight engineer Andy Goodall flew most of his time in JM671 with an Australian, F/Lt Bill Sprott, as skipper. His 'Cook's tour' of West African locations included Jui, Freetown, Sierra Leone; Fishlake, Liberia; Lagos, Nigeria; Port Etienne, Mauretania; Dakar, Senegal, and Bathurst, Gambia. Apart from anti-submarine patrols - and one attack on a suspected U-Boat - Sprott's crew was also tasked with escorting an Admiralty dock; searching for a missing boom defence vessel and an air-sea rescue for two missing Marauder bombers.
WING COMMANDER STAN BAGGOTT COLLECTION

Air to Air... A fine study of Mark III DV963, the usual 95 Squadron mount of Philip Christopher and crew in 1944/45. This aircraft spent two years in squadron service - but nearly didn't make it! In January 1943, on its long delivery flight from Gibraltar to Freetown and with fuel exhausted, F/O Jack Welton and crew successfully ditched between Freetown and Bathurst. They had been airborne for 17 hours, 45 minutes - a remarkable feat for a Sunderland. Crewman Bill Wood remembers that after several hours of waiting, help came in the form of a RAF air-sea rescue launch and finally a tow from a RAF pinnace into Jui. Rochester-built, DV963 served until the war's end before returning to the UK. It was apparently bought back by Short Brothers in June 1945.
PHILIP CHRISTOPHER

Censored... The ASV radar aerials on the Sunderland have been crudely censored in this photo of 95 Squadron personnel at Bathurst. The date is September 1943 and 171 officers and men, plus some 'locals', make up the group. The CO at the time was W/Cdr P. R. Hatfield, who was awarded a DFC for his work with the squadron. Those in the second row from the front have been named. Left to right: F/O Scott-Forrest; F/O Bob Watson; F/O Stoddart; F/O Bert Rich; F/O Ogilvie; F/O Searle; F/Lt Bill Sprott; F/Lt Simon Rowan; F/O Freddie Field; F/O 'Lord' Catip; F/Lt Rogers; F/Lt 'Happy' Adams, DFC; S/L Raban (flight commander); W/Cdr Hatfield DFC (CO); F/O Merrall (Adjutant); F/Lt Kitto; F/Lt Mack; F/O Bice; F/O Don Curran; F/O Honey; F/O Dunnett; F/O Gunn; P/O Wigley; F/O Philip Christopher; F/O Bob Russell; F/O Shields.
PHILIP CHRISTOPHER / IAN PATON

'Archimedes'... Close inshore for repairs near Port Etienne, Mauretania, in May 1943 is 95 Squadron's EJ144 - carrying the name 'Archimedes II' above the port doorway. 'Archimedes' joined the squadron in January 1943 and was damaged in a forced landing, losing its port float. Repairs were effected and EJ144 flew again, only to sink during a squall at Bathurst in October the following year. The vertical radar aerials above the fuselage have been painted out by the censor but other aerials have not been given the same treatment. *STEVE ELLAMS*

In distress... Two photographs of West African Sunderlands in distress. The half submerged aircraft is JM680, of 204 Squadron, which came to grief at the oddy-named Half Die on May 31st 1943 after hitting another Sunderland, W6062, on take off. The other aircraft, showing heavy damage to its port wing and tail fin, is almost certainly W6062, of 95 Squadron. JM680 managed to take off, even thought it had sustained a large hole in the hull, and fuel and depth charges were jettisoned before landing. It sank in seconds but with no crew injuries. For the record, JM680 was salvaged but then written off while W6062 was struck off charge in November 1943. *BOTH STEVE ELLAMS*

Latitudes... Reinforcements for the West African air patrols came in the form of 204 Squadron's Sunderlands, switched from chilly northern latitudes of the Shetlands and Iceland to equatorial Africa. The squadron's first aircraft arrived at Bathurst at the end of August 1941 and 204 remained in the theatre for the rest of the war. Here 204 Squadron's aircrew line up for a squadron photograph at Bathurst, using the same Sunderland as its sister squadron, No 95 (see Page 31).
In September 1943, when the photograph was taken, 204 changed COs with W/Cdr C. E. V. Evison handing over to W/Cdr H. J. L. Hawkins. During its time in West Africa 204 made two U-Boat attacks and carried out the multitude of tasks which flying-boats could uniquely perform. The squadron disbanded at Jui on June 30th 1945.
RON BIRCHALL

Conversion... In late 1943 No 270 Squadron at Jui began converting from Catalinas to Sunderlands, becoming an all-Sunderland unit by the following May. EK584, a Mark III built by Blackburns, was one of its aircraft. For the last few months of the war meteorological flights formed much of the squadron's task and it disbanded at Apapa, Lagos, on June 30th 1945. EK584 had earlier returned to the UK for allocation to 308 Ferry Training Unit and was disposed of in June 1945.
HARWOOD COLLECTION
via DERIC BROCK

Mind the trees!...
A Sunderlander's view of RAF Apapa, the Nigerian base which was familiar territory to all who served on 270 Squadron.
One who remembers it well is Ron White. "We used to take off from left to right and there were trees at the far end which we just managed to clear. The land drome was ex-BOAC and we were billeted in some of the old buildings," he recalled.
RON WHITE

Beached... An accident at Port Lyautey, Morocco, delayed the return home of Mark III ML849, until recently with 270 Squadron. In the crew was newly qualified first pilot Mac Bettjeman together with the captain, S/Ldr Sandy Powell, and squadron CO, W/Cdr Hall. Mac remembered: "On 11th June 1945 we departed Jui for Port Etienne and did the hop to Port Lyautey on the 14th. On June 16th ML849 was taxied out to the straight stretch of river used as a seaplane alighting area. The river was quite narrow and when we were half way round the wind caught us and the full blast of both motors failed to bring us around in time. We watched helplessly as our starboard float crumpled on the bank. Frantic efforts were made to get some crew members out of the top hatch and onto the port wing but we were not in time to prevent the wingtip becoming immersed in the river. It took an alarming number of sandbags to lift up the wing and the aircraft was towed to a jetty and moored alongside with the starboard wing extending across the jetty." Over the coming days the Sunderland was a big draw for airmen belonging to a United States B-17 bomber squadron located nearby, the usual question being: 'Gee, does this thing fly?' Indeed it did. A new float was flown in from Gibraltar and the repaired Sunderland continued its journey home on July 1st flying into Mount Batten and then on to Wig Bay. Another member of the crew, Brian Hanson, recalled that this was Powell's only 'prang' in 1,200 hours of flying. Blackburn-built ML849 joined 270 Squadron in April 1944, being flown from Oban's Ferry Training Unit by W/O Einarson, RCAF, and crew. Flight engineer Bob Elrick logged a 17-day flight via Pembroke Dock, Gibraltar, Bathurst and Jui before reaching Apapa, Lagos. ML849 languished in store at Wig Bay, Stranraer, after its return, its official demise being 'sold for scrap' in March 1947.
MAC BETTJEMAN

Kiwi kite... Tucked in close to a sister aircraft is ML810, one of the Kiwi kites of No 490 Squadron. A Belfast-built Mark III, ML810 joined 490 in May 1944 and just over a year later was struck off charge, days before the squadron disbanded on August 1st 1945. It was the last of the West Africa squadron to disband, their jobs well and truly done.
AIR FORCE MUSEUM, CHRISTCHURCH, NEW ZEALAND 040135

Flying the flag... Proudly flying the flag at RAF Jui are officers of No 490 Squadron in March 1945. One of seven Royal New Zealand Air Force squadrons to form within the wartime RAF, 490 initially equipped with Catalinas but Sunderlands arrived in May 1944, taking over the long and mostly unproductive routine patrols. The squadron's last CO, W/Cdr T. F. Gill, joined his officers for the group photo - all have been named (left to right).
Back row: F/Lt Waring, F/O Pierce, F/O Fitzmay, P/O McPherson, P/O Hall, F/O Alty, F/O Verscheffelt, P/O McEwan, F/O Broughton, F/Lt Wheeler, F/O Johnson, F/Lt Cowtan, F/Lt Watt, F/O Anderson.
Middle: P/O Everson, F/O Simpson, F/O Sly, F/Lt Wilson, F/Lt Emmanuel, P/O Lee, F/Lt Angelo, F/Lt Labes, F/Lt Calquohoun, F/Lt Houtheusen, F/O Stratton, P/O Holloway, F/Lt Ellis, F/Lt Davis, P/O Blackman, P/O Martin, F/Lt Dominey.
Front: F/Lt Heggie, F/Lt Brabbon, F/Lt Hariman, F/O McGreal, F/Lt Patterson, F/Lt King, F/Lt Roberts (MO), F/Lt Sherwell, S/Ldr Dunn (flight commander), W/Cdr Gill (CO), S/Ldr Kilgour (chief flying instructor), F/Lt Birch (adjutant), F/Lt Howley, F/Lt Augost, F/Lt Wright, F/Lt Henderson, F/O Simpson, F/Lt McDonald, F/Lt Peterson.
AIR FORCE MUSEUM, CHRISTCHURCH, NEW ZEALAND 940213

Groundcrew... Conditions for the long enduring groundcrews who maintained the Sunderlands in West African locations were always harsh and difficult. This anonymous Mark III of 490 Squadron, possibly carrying the identity letter K, is seen at RAF Jui.
HAROLD MARTIN

Chapter V La Reine d'Hydravions

France was a long time operator of the Sunderland, acquiring the first examples in 1943 and continuing right up to the early 1960s. Following the Allied invasion of North Africa in 1943 Sunderlands began re-equipping local flying-boat units which became Escadrille 7E at Dakar in mid 1943, retitling as 7FE (Flottille d'Exploration) in the October. Another change on paper came in November 1943 when No 343 Squadron RAF came into being. In all, 25 Sunderlands flew with French units up to the end of the war, six being lost in that time. In November 1945, the war over, No 343 Squadron transferred to the Aeronavale, being retitled Flottille 7FE with Dakar still its main base. It subsequently became 7F and later 27F. Post-war another 25 Sunderlands from RAF stocks joined the French Navy, the last five as late as 1957 as the RAF were pensioning off their remaining examples.

The following four photographs are reproduced courtesy Association pour la Recherche de Documentation sue l'Historie de l'Aeronautique Navale (ARDHAN). They appear in the book 'L'Aeronautique Navale Francaise au Royaume-uni'. With acknowledgement to M. Jean-Marie Commeau.

Kitted out... A formal photograph of tropically kitted-out aircrew in front of Mark III ML871, seen at Dakar in 1944. ML871, a Blackburn example, joined 343 Squadron in July 1944 after service with 422 (Canadian) Squadron. It went on to fly in French Navy colours before being struck off charge in November 1950.
ARDHAN

Grim toll... After brief allocation to 461 Squadron, RAAF, Mark III DV865 flew out to Africa in the late summer of 1943 for service with 7FE and then 343 Squadron. Its loss on 26th April the following year in a crash off Goree Island brought with it the grim toll of 13 airmen killed.
ARDHAN

Unsung... Just two of the Mark IIIs which did sterling but unsung service with the French in African skies.

Right: One of 35 Sunderlands built at the Shorts factory at Windermere, DP187 joined 343 Squadron in October 1943 and continued with Aeronavale post war. It was disposed of in June 1947.
ARDHAN

Below: DV987, seen patrolling off Senegal in 1944, only lasted until just after the end of the war against Germany. It joined 343 Squadron in September 1943 and was struck off charge in June 1945.
ARDHAN

Reinforcement... First of the post-war batches of Mark V Sunderlands to reinforce the French Navy was ML750, taking up its new colours in July 1947. It had previously seen wartime service - as a Mark III - with 422 Squadron, RCAF. Its new career was short, being written off after a ground accident at Dakar in July 1950.
Via J. Cuny/Chaz Bowyer.

Veteran... Among the last five Sunderlands allocated to France in 1957 was SZ571, a Belfast-built RAF veteran. This had seen extensive RAF service post war, including with 201, 209, 205 and 88 Squadrons. It soldiered on with Aeronavale and was one of the last to be struck off charge, in April 1961.
Via J. Cuny/Chaz Bowyer.

For Generations to Come

Four-engined disco!... After peacetime service with the French Navy, Mark V ML796 was called up for a unique role - that of restaurant and discotheque, complete with spiral staircase! For some years ML796 was a very familiar and unusual roadside sight at La Baule, Brittany, but over the years the elements - and later vandalism - took their toll. When acquired by the Imperial War Museum in 1975 ML796 was in a very sorry state.

Pieter Kroon took on the challenging task of rescuing the Sunderland, having already recovered a B-17 Flying Fortress for the Imperial War Museum two years earlier.

Pieter remembered: "On arrival at La Baule the owner and his wife took me to see the Sunderland. Its condition was much poorer for transportation by road than expected. Access was by means of a ladder and .... it was immediately obvious that literally anybody had been able to get in and take what they pleased. The spiral staircase was still in place and so was the main floor; both virtually holding the aircraft together and upright. Doors and windows were missing all round - but not the toilet pot in the front!"

It was decided to remove the wings, tail and floats and slice the fuselage in half horizontally and all the pieces were skillfully accommodated on three large lorries.

The story of the remarkable recovery of a very weathered and battered aircraft would fill a booklet in itself. An export licence had to be obtained for a 'warplane', along with 'Convoi Exceptional' permits from the many Departements along the route for the passage of these huge loads.

"Travelling through many different city and village police areas, we often had to wait a considerable time to be handed over from one police escort to another which gave local spectators an excellent opportunity to view the Sunderland's progress," Pieter recalled. "The journey from La Baule to Dunkirk took three and a half days, including through the city of Rouen as the ring road was closed."

Seven days after leaving its last resting place ML796 began the final stretch of its journey, from Harwich to Duxford.

"The welcome given to the Sunderland was somewhat emotional, not in the least because it was clear to all concerned how daunting the task of restoring ML796 would be in the years to come. Now everyone visiting Duxford can see the result of the many years of hard work put into the refurbishment of the Sunderland - a job well worth doing."

Bottom: A treasured reminder of Pieter Kroon's key involvement in ML796's return to the UK is this postcard view of the Sunderland in its hey-day as a restaurant. This was given to him by the last owner just before the convoy of lorries left La Baule.
Via PIETER KROON

Before... Two photos showing the sorry state of ML796 before it was removed to Duxford.
BOTH PIETER KROON

After... In all its glory - ML796 following restoration. It is one of just three military Sunderlands preserved in the world. The others are at the RAF Museum, Hendon, London (Mark V ML824) and at the Museum of Transport and Technology, Auckland, New Zealand (Mark V NZ4115, formerly SZ584).
PIETER KROON

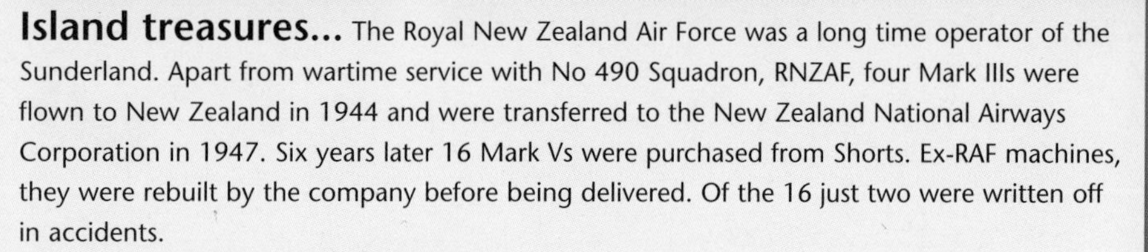

Island treasures... The Royal New Zealand Air Force was a long time operator of the Sunderland. Apart from wartime service with No 490 Squadron, RNZAF, four Mark IIIs were flown to New Zealand in 1944 and were transferred to the New Zealand National Airways Corporation in 1947. Six years later 16 Mark Vs were purchased from Shorts. Ex-RAF machines, they were rebuilt by the company before being delivered. Of the 16 just two were written off in accidents.

In November 1959 NZ4111 (ex-VB880) hit an underwater obstruction in the Te Whanga Lagoon in the Chatham Islands. The crew beached the aircraft and later its engines and all salvageable equipment were recovered.

The other accident involved NZ4117 (ex-RN286) which was damaged landing in rough seas at Tarawa, in the Gilbert and Ellis Islands, in April 1961. Later the Sunderland was flown to Fiji where the decision was made to reduce it to spares.

For over 30 years substantial parts of NZ4111 remained where they had been abandoned in the Chatham Islands - but they were not forgotten. In the early 1990s the RNZAF mounted a recovery operation which resulted in many parts being brought back to be displayed at the RNZAF Museum in Christchurch.

Top: NZ4111, its fuselage broken and without engines, during salvage work at Te Whanga Lagoon, March 1960. Its long part-immersion in the lagoon shows up on the fuselage side.
Above Left: The cockpit section looms out of the undergrowth, December 1993.
Above Right: A float, front turret and other items on display at the RNAF Museum in 1996.
AIR FORCE MUSEUM, CHRISTCHURCH, NEW ZEALAND, WH G1692, 9617220 and 961881

Chapter VI Fly East

Sunderlands operated in the Far East from the earliest days of RAF service. No 230 Squadron received its first Sunderlands at Seletar in June 1938 and over the next 19 years several other units would operate the type in eastern skies, in wartime and peacetime conditions. Fittingly, it was at Seletar that the last of a long line of Sunderlands in RAF roundels would grace the skies before being pensioned off after a then record period of active service for one aircraft type.

Tasks... Just two of 230's hard working aircraft as the squadron tackled many tasks in various locations. In the air is EJ141, a Rochester-built Mark III, while 'M' is almost certainly JM711. After serving with 230, EJ141 transferred to 205 Squadron and while on a non-operational flight in March 1945 the port inner engine failed, leading to a forced landing in the Maldive Islands. The aircraft was struck off charge in the June - whether as a result of the incident in the Maldives is not clear. As for JM711 it was involved in an accident when landing in the Scillies in August 1943, the port float hitting a boat at the end of a ferry flight. Then with the Ferry Training Unit at Pembroke Dock, JM711 was soon repaired and headed east to 230 Squadron, later joining the Iraq Communications Flight. It was disposed of, most likely in that area, in August 1946. The common practice was the remove useful equipment and then quietly sink the aircraft in deep water.
BOTH WING COMMANDER DUNDAS BEDNALL

'British Here'... 230 Squadron Sunderland crews flying over the Burmese city of Rangoon - so recently in Japanese control - were given a stark reminder of the human cost of the bitter war in the Far East. The words 'British Here' could be made out on a roof of this prisoner of war camp in the city. The flight was made in May 1945.
S. J. 'PADDY' MAXWELL

Depot ship... *HMS Manela*, a familiar shape to many flying-boat crews in World War II. Officially a 'seaplane depot ship', *Manela* was completed on the Clyde in 1921 and had an earlier life as a passenger cargo ship on the Karachi-Bombay and later the Calcutta-Australia routes before being called up by the Royal Navy in October 1939. At the outbreak of war *Manela* was at Sullom Voe in the Shetlands, a floating base for 201 Squadron's London flying-boats, and moved to Iceland later to support 204 Squadron. Transferred to RAF Coastal Command control in October 1941, the 8,303 ton *Manela* headed for West African waters - at a top speed of 13 knots - in support of the Sunderland squadrons there and moved eastward as the tides of war spread. This picture was taken in 1945 when *Manela* was at Syriam, Burma, in support of 230 Squadron. When the war ended this war-weary veteran had one last task to perform - transporting troops and former prisoners-of-war home. In July 1946, after 25 years of service, this venerable lady was towed to the Netherlands for scrapping.
FRED WHITE via JIM BRISLEY/PETER GRAY

Back at Seletar... 230 Squadron returned to pre-war haunts at Singapore as the war ended and one of its new Mark Vs, PP154, is pictured at anchor in the Jahore Straits. PP154, among the first batch of Mark Vs built by Blackburn, had a post war career serving also with 205 and 209 Squadrons in the early 1950s. It was struck off charge in September 1957, along with many of its sisters. *PETER GRAY*

Brief encounter... In 1945, amid hopes that the war would soon be ending, a number of RAF squadrons converted from Catalinas to Sunderlands. No 212 Squadron may well have followed this course but it was not to be. PP126 is thought to be the only Sunderland taken on squadron charge (in June) before the unit re-numbered as 240 Squadron at Redhills Lake, Madras, on July 1st. For the next few months PP126 flew on with 240 until the squadron disbanded at Koggala. It was struck off charge, at least on paper, in August 1947. *212 SQUADRON ARCHIVES /ANDY THOMAS COLLECTION*

Norse name... Harking back to its associations with Iceland in the early part of the war, 240 Squadron adopted a winged helmet for its Badge. In an adaption, one of the squadron's Sunderlands carried the helmet and the Norse name 'Thor'. *J. H. BATCHELOR*

Signing off... Koggala in Ceylon was 240 Squadron's final flying-boat station, signing off there in March 1946 with a group photograph in front of one of their Sunderlands. The CO was W/Cdr C. B. Gavin Robinson AFC.
KEN ROBINSON/TERRY MARTIN /J. H. BATCHELOR

Short lived...

No 259 Squadron's wartime beat was in Indian Ocean skies, for all but a month of active duty with the Catalina. In March 1945 it began to convert to Sunderlands but a month later these were transferred to No 35 Squadron, South African Air Force, and 259 disbanded on April 30th. PP153, its first Sunderland, is pictured off Mombassa. It's service with the SAAF was incredibly brief - being written off in an accident within 24 hours.
PETER TEBBITT /ANDY THOMAS COLLECTION

Heritage...

Squadrons don't come with any finer flying-boat heritage that No 205. Its lineage dates back to the Far East Flight of 1927 and it served for 30 years on 'boats. Its Sunderland chapter began in June 1945 at Koggala, Ceylon, where RN301/D was photographed late that year. A Blackburn-built Mark V, RN301 only served with 205. Officially it was struck off charge in 1951.
G. COLE

Repeat... In an unusual departure from the 'norm', the serial of Mark V PP123 is repeated in front of the fin flash. R-Robert was on 205 Squadron's books at the time, subsequently returning to the UK. Its RAF service ended prematurely in December 1948 when it sank at Wig Bay, Stranraer, during a gale.
Via DAVID NEVILLE

All stripes... An all-NCO crew serving with 205 Squadron photographed at RAAF Iwakuni, Japan, in November 1950. All have been named (left to right): Standing, F/Sgt 'Tubby' Taylor (signaller), F/Sgt Sam Worthington (engineer), Sgt Archie Kinch (captain), Sgt Sandy Crooke (engineer), Sgt 'Taffy' Poyntz (co-pilot); Front: Sgt MacDonald (signaller), F/Sgt 'Dobie' Dobson (air gunner), S/Sgt Ken Burlton (navigator).
SQUADRON LEADER ARCHIE KINCH

Tropical... A fine study of 205 Squadron's PP137, showing marks on the hull from immersions in tropical waters. One of the last batch of Mark IIIs off the Blackburn production line, PP137 was soon upgraded to Mark V status and served with 4 OTU before joining 205 in May 1953. It remustered with 205/209 Squadron before being struck off charge in early 1957.
BILL DEVINE

Cameo... PP151 is the centre of attention under the high sun when with its only frontline unit, 209 Squadron. The location is probably Koggala. Another squadron with a splendid flying-boat pedigree, 209 had a succession of 'boats from 1930 until 1955 when it merged with 205 Squadron but the number lived on in the squadron title until the end of the Sunderland era. PP151's operational time over, it was plucked from storage to perform a cameo role as a trials aircraft, being modified with an enlarged fin as part of tests for the Short Sperrin jet bomber. With its strange new look it flew for Shorts at Belfast between November 1950 and May the following year. Further long term storage followed before the inevitable scrapping, its struck off charge date being October 1956.
MRS MARY WILSON

Codes...

Carrying the code letters WQ, two of 209 Squadron's early Sunderlands are seen in characteristic poses.

Right is SZ565, S-Sugar, overflying the North Borneo jungle. A Belfast-built example, SZ565 later flew with 201 Squadron before taking a training role with 235 Operational Conversion Unit, based at Calshot. It was while operating with the OCU in November 1951 that SZ565 was lost in a crash landing off Hillhead, Hampshire. The two pilots died.
RON LAWRENCE

Bottom: NJ265, part of a neat line up, exhibits another variation on a markings theme - the repeat of the serial number below the fin flash. NJ265 later returned to the UK and was also used by 235 OCU at Calshot. It was struck off charge in August 1955.
PETER TEBBITT via DR ARTHUR BANKS

Engine ahoy...

An engine change on the water is in progress for SZ560 at China Bay, Ceylon. This Mark V saw service with 205 and 209 Squadrons in the east and back in the UK with the Flying-Boat Training Squadron and 230 Squadron at Pembroke Dock.
It was struck off charge in October 1957.
RAY LOCK

Keep 'em flying...

An immaculately turned out group in front of one of their charges. This is the Far East Flying-Boat Wing Repair and Servicing personnel photographed in 1952 or 1953. Without the efforts of the ground staff no flying-boats would ever have operated.
ALLEN WILLIAMS

Webfoot world... A famous wartime bomber squadron number transferred into the webfoot world in September 1946 when No 1430 transport flight at Kai Tak, Hong Kong, was numbered No 88 Squadron. The squadron was engaged in transport and courier duties between Far Eastern bases, becoming a general reconnaissance unit and going to war during the Korean Conflict. In June 1951 it relocated to Seletar, Singapore, and disbanded there in October 1954. Pictured are squadron aircrew in 1949-50 with the CO, S/Ldr Duggie Gall.
SQUADRON LEADER DICK DULIEU

In pirate country!... In January 1949, 88 Squadron provided essential support for a most unusual rescue effort which thankfully ended successfully. A Vampire jet of a RAF trials unit force landed out of fuel on a remote island in Bias Bay, near Hong Kong - in Chinese waters and an area noted for its pirates! Before long 88's F/Lt Ken Letford and crew located the undamaged jet and landed to provide initial help. This was the beginning of a remarkable joint service effort which finally saw the jet taken onto a landing craft and then winched aboard the Royal Navy cruiser, *HMS Belfast*. Another 88 Squadron Sunderland, NJ176, piloted by the CO, S/Ldr Gall and F/O Dilieu, can be seen in the background as RAF and Navy personnel prepare to uplift the jet. Vampire pilot F/Lt George 'Kiwi' Francis, made a masterly dead stick landing and his aircraft was soon flying again.
KEN FOSTER via SQUADRON LEADER DICK DILIEU

Medal... Nose down in the shallows at Seletar is 88 Squadron's NJ176, the sad aftermath of a night take off accident in November 1949 during a thunderstorm. Several of the crew were trapped in the wreckage and heroic rescue efforts were made to save them. The senior station medical officer at RAF Seletar, S/Ldr Robert Ellis Woolley, was subsequently awarded the George Medal for extricating two seriously injured crewmen. Throughout the rescue there was constant danger of spilt fuel igniting. Sadly the pilot and four others died as a result of the accident. At the time NJ176 had been carrying eight crew and four passengers. In addition to S/Ldr Woolley, another medical officer and three airmen received King's Commendations for Brave Conduct.
ALEX CARRIE

Detachment... The sign by the squadron offices says it all - the Sunderland's final days in RAF service was as part of the detachment of 205/209 Squadron at RAF Seletar.
ALEX CARRIE

Write off... Recently arrived ML745 was damaged beyond repair in 1957 after slipping off its tail trolley. The hull rests on the tarmac and the ripples in the aircraft's skin tell their own story.
ALEX CARRIE

Top brass... The Air Officer Commanding at Singapore, Air Marshal the Earl of Bandon, joined the crew for the final official flight by a Sunderland in RAF service on May 20th 1959. He is pictured with staff and the crew of ML797 (all left to right). Back row: F/Lt Adcock (flight engineer); ? (OC Marine Craft Section); S/Ldr Reed; W/Cdr ? ; F/Lt Jack Poyser (captain and OC 205 Squadron Sunderland Detachment); ? ; W/Cdr R. A. N. McReady (OC 205 Shackleton Squadron and a former Sunderlander); Air Marshal the Earl of Bandon; G/Capt Hooper (OC RAF Seletar); ?. Front row: F/Sgt Barnes (signaller); F/Sgt Bevis (signaller); Sgt O'Leary (flight engineer); F/Lt Ben Ford (co-pilot); F/Lt French (navigator); F/L Josey (signaller).
JACK POYSER

The end... Stripped of engines, turrets, floats and all useful equipment, ML797 - a history-making Sunderland - awaits the inevitable in the Seletar scrapyard.
DOUG HOGGARTH via JOHN BRIGNELL

Chapter VII Peacetime at PD

Everyday... A once everyday and so familiar scene - white-hulled Sunderlands at their moorings off Pembroke Dock. Flying-boats and PD will forever be linked in history. The Pembrokeshire town, on the shores of the magnificent Milford Haven Waterway, was a flying-boat station for nearly 30 years. And for 19 of those years the waterfront echoed to the sounds of the mighty Sunderlands as they went about their daily business. PD became the last of the UK flying-boat stations to fly the RAF Ensign. From 1949 until 1957 it was home base to Nos 201 and 230 Squadrons - the last units to operate the Sunderland in the UK. This photograph was taken towards the end of Pembroke Dock's illustrious flying-boat era. It seemed as if Sunderlands would always be the backdrop to PD's daily life - and then, almost overnight, they were gone. A very special era had ended, but PD's place in history was assured.
VIC BENSON

Long service...
The Sunderland was operated by the RAF for 21 years and for all but two of those years it was 230 Squadron's workhorse. The squadron took delivery of its first Mark Is in 1938 and was flying Mark Vs in 1957 when it disbanded along with sister squadron, No 201. Here 230 Squadron personnel - plus dog - pose in front of RN304 at Pembroke Dock, 1951.
PETER CONNOLLY

Erratum

The group photo (Page 51) is now known to have been taken at Calshot in mid 1951 and is of the station personnel plus staff, instructors and students of No 235 OCU. The error will be corrected in the next edition.

Further information has come to light on the picture (Page 63) of the salvaged Sunderland. This is now believed to be ML829 of 10 Squadron, RAAF, which crashed at Plymouth on 9th February 1945 with the loss of two crew.

Paterchurch Publications, *6 Laws Street, Pembroke Dock, SA72 6DL*

Goodwill... The crew of RN304 of 230 Squadron photographed before a goodwill visit to Stavangar, Norway, in August 1951. They were joined by three ground staff (back row) who have not been identified. Front row, left to right: P/O Jock Beer, F/Lt Ian Bergh, F/Lt Tom Holland, F/O Jeff Jeavons. Middle row, left to right: F/Sgt Kay, Sgt ?, Sgt Manobier, Pilot II Jones, F/Sgt ?
PETER CONNOLLY

Album... One for the squadron album - No 201's officers line up in a formal group, perhaps before the Squadron moved to PD in 1949. Many of the faces have been named (all left to right): Back row: F/O Davies, F/O Allin, ? , ? , F/Lt Ludlam, ? , P/O Gilbert, F/O Hardy, F/O Busby, ? , P/O Bartrum, P/O Cann, ? , ? , P/O Rhodes, ? , ? , F/Lt Aylward.
Middle row: ? , F/O Brown, F/Lt Whitmore, F/Lt Nicoll, F/Lt Stavert, F/Lt Gill, F/O Oldfield, F/Lt Cassels, F/Lt Webster, F/Lt Prior, F/O Angell, F/O Lister, F/Lt Bartley, F/Lt Baker, F/O Witter, F/Lt Wilkinson, F/Lt Ford, F/Lt Hall, ?.
Front row: F/Lt Pearse, F/Lt Whittaker, F/Lt Wilson, F/Lt Gibbons, F/Lt Fenton, S/Ldr Austin, S/Ldr Rumbold, W/Cdr Heath, G/Capt Turner, S/Ldr Fegen, ? , S/Ldr Dagger, F/Lt McLoughlin, ? , F/Lt Hackman, F/Lt Mathews, F/Lt Fenton.
IAN WITTER

Union Jack... As befitting a 'ship' in a foreign port, Sunderland A-Able of 201 Squadron flies the Union Jack during a visit to Norway - probably soon after the war had ended. This is PP144, a Blackburn-built example, which joined 201 in June 1945 but its time on the squadron was short. Later PP144 flew with 205 and 88 Squadrons out East before returning to the UK and a date with the scrapman in 1955.
GROUP CAPTAIN J. W. LOUW COLLECTION

Air-to-air... Fine studies of two of 230 Squadron's peacetime Sunderlands, very likely taken around the same time. **Below left** is JM718 which began life as a Mark III off the Rochester production line. It was held back from wartime squadron service for a secret trials role (see Chapter VIII) and did not finally join 230 until February 1950, moving on to 235 OCU. A further spell with 230 came in October 1954 and this photograph was taken in August the following year with F/O Nicholas as captain. At the time the PD squadrons were preparing for a royal flypast to mark the Queen's visit to Pembrokeshire. JM718 went into storage in early 1957 and was scrapped before the end of the year.

Above: SZ567 tucked in very close. Belfast-built, SZ567 was too late for war service but did a long stint in 230's colours in the mid 1950s, including participation in RAF Pembroke Dock's support of the British North Greenland Expedition. Struck off charge/scrap was the fate of this peacetime veteran.
JOHN LEEKS and RAY 'MONTY' HUMBLE

Feature... For one of its issues in the early 1950s 'Flight' magazine featured the work of the flying-boat units at PD. This informal line up of 201 Squadron, with over 80 personnel, was used to illustrate the article. Six Sunderlands ride at their moorings behind. At the time S/Ldr P. A. S. Rumbold was squadron CO.
FLIGHT 266705 via ANDREW EDNEY

Dog carrier... Resting at a Pembroke Dock mooring is VB889, the last of 240 Sunderlands built under licence at the Blackburn's factory at Dumbarton. First flown in November 1945 it was later allocated to 201 Squadron and took up the individual letter D. This was especially appropriate when, in the summer of 1954, D-Dog was loaned to 230 Squadron to help bring home the North Greenland Expedition. The expedition's pack of huskies was also brought back - and 230 wisely earmarked D-Dog of its sister squadron to be the dog carrier. After the long flight, with stopovers, from Greenland to Pembroke Dock D-Dog lived up to more than its name! One of the last ever Sunderlands could have been a candidate for preservation, but it was not to be. VB889, last of the Dumbarton line and dog carrier, was sold for scrap in September 1957.
MRS WINNIE BEST

Battle of Britain... Each September in the 1950s, until the Sunderlands were retired, an example from home-based units was flown to the Thames and moored up near Tower Bridge as part of celebrations to mark the anniversary of the Battle of Britain. In September 1953 it was the turn of RN290, carrying the B-Z codes of 230 Squadron. In January the following year RN290 was lost following an emergency landing at Angle Bay, near Pembroke Dock. An in-flight fire led to a rapid downwind landing and an even more rapid exit by the seven-man crew as the fire took hold of the aircraft. F/O B. S. M. Jones and his crew were rescued from the icy waters without serious injury but RN290 burnt out and sank. Five of the crew were picked up by another Sunderland, skippered by F/O D. A. Austin, which was taxied to the area. The other two were plucked from near the blazing aircraft by a Marine Craft Section launch.
JERRY MORBEY

Streamlined... The streamlined look of the 'Queen of the 'Boats' is shown to advantage in this shot of RN299, of 230 Squadron, c 1953. Another from the Blackburn factory, RN299 served with both 230 and 201 Squadrons at PD and was scrapped in 1957.
ROLAND MONTAGUE

Awash... The fin and rudder and a section of starboard wing are all that remained above water after PP122 of 201 Squadron came to grief when on a flying visit to the squadron's affiliated island of Guernsey in September 1954. E-Easy sank after hitting a rock off St Peter Port and never flew again. PP122 features in happier circumstances on the cover.
GUERNSEY PRESS CO via LEN PARKER

Twilight days... The sun was high but it was twilight days for the RAF's Sunderlands in the mid 1950s. Late on in their long service career the home based squadrons adopted the squadron number on the fuselage. SZ575, a Short and Harlands-built Mark V, took on the letter E after joining 201 in February 1955. This was its last 'posting' in a varied career which included spells on the training circuit with 4 OTU and 235 OCU and a few months with 230 Squadron. SZ575 was one of several of the breed to be struck off charge in October 1957.
VIC BENSON

Chapter VIII Trialists and Trainers

Glimpse... Newly commissioned Pilot Officers Martin and Gooch get their first glimpses of the very new Sunderland on their arrival at Calshot in early 1939. One of the first of the breed was ashore on its beaching gear, parked alongside Scapa and Singapore III biplanes of the resident Flying-Boat Training Squadron.
WING COMMANDER DEREK MARTIN

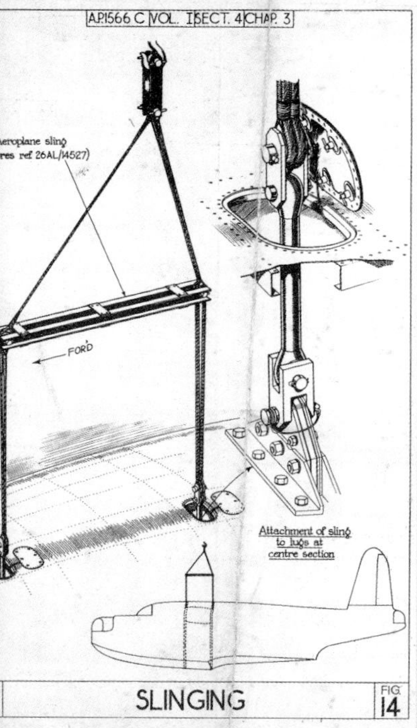

Hoisted high... The new Sunderland came complete with attachments for hoisting on a crane - it seems as though the designers had thought of everything. These fittings were soon put to the test, probably conducted at the Marine Aircraft and Experimental Establishment at Felixstowe, using the first production Sunderland, L2158.
BILL MORTIMER COLLECTION

Left: The official drawings showing how and where to 'sling' a Sunderland.
ERIC ODDY

Charioteer... Some of the most unusual trials carried out by Sunderlands involved attempts to transport 'chariots' - manned torpedoes - to high priority targets, the German battleship *Tirpitz*, sheltering in Norwegian fiords, being top of the hit list. The top secret project advanced to such a stage that no less than five Sunderlands were allocated for trials. These were Rochester-built Mark IIIs in the serial sequence JM714 to JM718 with '714 as the actual trials aircraft. Modifications were put in hand to attach the chariots in a cradle one each side of the Sunderland hull. All this took time and it was not until July 1943 that JM714 was delivered to the Marine Aircraft Experimental Establishment's wartime home at Helensburgh. The aircraft had the letter G - for guard - added to its serial number; all part of the security around these experiments.

On July 9th 1943 MAEE test pilot F/Lt Harold Pipes, accompanied by Sub Lt Lee, RN, an experienced charioteer, and a senior MAEE scientist, carried out the first successful handling trials in JM714. Days later two unarmed chariots were lifted into place and the aircraft flown to Bowmore on the Isle of Islay, a secluded location. Here the chariots were successfully lowered from the Sunderland and 'launched'. To prove the lifting capability of the Sunderland tests were carried out with lead ballast and full fuel load. Harold Pipes recalled that on July 30th he took off at an all up weight of 61,000 lbs in 83 seconds - this was 10,000 lb above normal maximum. The Sunderland was proving itself in yet another role.

However, the 'Charioteer' Sunderland never went to war - the trials were discontinued and the five special Sunderlands were stored at No 57 MU at Wig Bay. JM714 was sold back to Shorts in 1948 and converted into a Sandringham 6, going on to the Norwegian operator, DNL, as LN-LMK, and later to Aerolineas Argentinas as LV-PAE and then LV-AHM, named 'Admirante Zar'.

* The photograph is of JM714 during its record take off trials at Helensburgh in July 1943 with F/Lt Harold Pipes in command.

HAROLD PIPES

Anonymous... An unidentified Mark III up from Alness, home of No 4 Operational Training Unit where Sunderland crews formed up and completed their training prior to joining squadrons in various parts of the world.
JIM MEALOR

Sortie... Against a wooded landscape Mark III DD829 awaits its next training sortie at Lough Erne, Northern Ireland. The lower part of this lake became RAF Killadeas, the base of No 131 Operational Training Unit, and flying-boat crews trained here from mid 1942, initially with Catalinas and then Sunderlands too. DD829 spent 18 months with 201 Squadron before taking up a training role at Killadeas. After the war it went into storage and was scrapped in 1947.
GROUP CAPTAIN TOM HARVEY

Prototype... Taxiing in front of the famous Seaplane Works at Rochester is ML965, the prototype Mark V. The adoption of the American Pratt and Whitney Twin Wasp radials gave the Sunderland a new lease of life, allowing it to operate well beyond wartime days. Early in 1944 ML765 was taken from the Rochester line and fitted with 1,200 hp Twin Wasps. At the same time engineers with No 10 Squadron, RAAF, at Mount Batten, were carrying out a similar conversion on ML839, and both flew successfully. The Mark V was the last of the Sunderland line but ML765 did not survive long. After trials at MAEE it was returned to the RAF and struck off charge in November 1947.
MRS A. MAIN via HENRY ROLFE

Air day... An impressive sight at any air day - two Sunderlands, in close formation and very low. This was a highlight of the Battle of Britain display at West Freugh, the Royal Aircraft Establishment's Scottish outpost, in September 1954. Flying the leading Sunderland was Ben Ford with Fred Weaver in No2 position. Fred Weaver also did a low pass with only the port inner engine working - a master flying-boat pilot demonstrating the superb handling qualities and lack of vices of a remarkable aircraft. His particular aircraft for this display was SZ560.
SQUADRON LEADER FRED WEAVER

Test team... As Sunderlands were brought out of storage at Wig Bay, Stranraer, in the 1950s they were tested by a small RAF team, working alongside the Short Brothers contractors who ran what was formerly No 57 Maintenance Unit. Here members of both teams join for an informal photograph. The RAF personnel have been named (all left to right). Back row: Shorts representative, F/Sgt John Bishop, F/O Fred Weaver. Front row: Two Shorts representatives, F/Sgt Smith, F/Sgt Hawthorne and F/Sgt Brooks.
SQUADRON LEADER FRED WEAVER

History... Carrying the TA codes of No 4 OTU, ML778 is just another Sunderland earning its keep as a trainer. But this one came with a bit of history. In June 1945, this aircraft - then with 201 Squadron based at Castle Archdale - flew Coastal Command's last wartime convoy patrol. The war had been over for nearly a month but convoy patrols continued until the position regarding the remaining German U-Boats had been established. ML778 only joined 201 in May and by early July it had moved on to the Operational Training Unit at Alness. Lengthy storage followed before ML778 was picked for French Navy service, taking up its new colours in 1951. The final curtain came after an accident in July 1958 and this history-making Sunderland was struck off charge by its French owners.
MAP

Swansong... RN303 sits on its beaching gear at Pembroke Dock, one of the last to serve at PD. The D in the coding indicates an aircraft of the Flying-Boat Training Squadron which latterly had undertaken the training of crews on station. Unlike others pensioned off in 1957, RN303 did have another life, being sent down the line to Seletar, Singapore, to join the last operator, No 205/209 Squadron, for the Sunderlands' swansong in RAF markings. In its advancing years RN303 appears to have picked up some bad habits because it was not popular with its new owners and was classed as a 'rogue' aircraft. Such aircraft are quickly disposed of and RN303 was struck off charge in January 1959.
RAY EVANS

Chapter IX Casualties

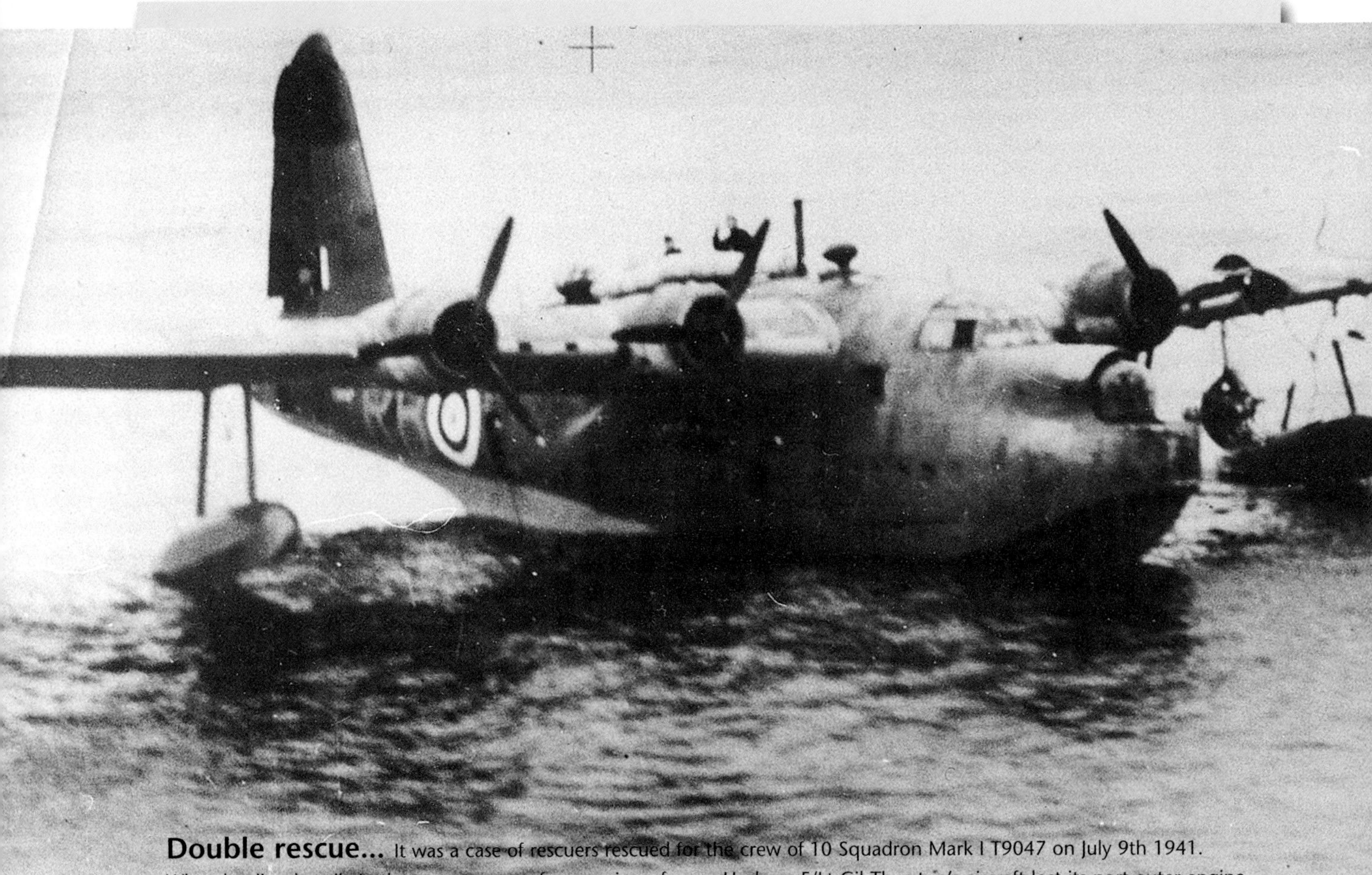

Double rescue... It was a case of rescuers rescued for the crew of 10 Squadron Mark I T9047 on July 9th 1941. When landing heavily in the open sea near four survivors from a Hudson, F/Lt Gil Thurstun's aircraft lost its port outer engine which fell out of it housing. The Hudson crew were taken aboard and the Sunderland remained firmly waterborne. Using the three remaining engines the Sunderland was taxied towards the Scilly Isles and eventually rescue came in the form of *HMS Brocklesby*. All the airmen were taken aboard the destroyer and the Sunderland was sunk by gunfire - a sad finale to a long saga. The only casualties were the Sunderland's two homing pigeons. They had been released with messages after the landing but never returned to base.
WING COMMANDER VIC HODGKINSON

Exercise... The remains of Mark III W6028 lie in the Fermanagh countryside, a tragic ending to a fighter affiliation exercise involving the 422 Squadron aircraft and crew. Operating from Castle Archdale in February 1944 the Sunderland was working with Beaufighters from St Angelo, another Northern Ireland air station. Of the crew, eight were injured and two lost their lives.
422 SQUADRON ASSOCIATION

Tragic sequence... Emerging from the depths at Plymouth Harbour is the battered remains of ML782, a Mark III operated by 228 Squadron. Diverted to Mount Batten on December 10th 1944, the aircraft crashed on landing, with the loss of two crew. This, sadly, was only the beginning of a tragic sequence of events. A civilian salvage company was called in and the Sunderland was raised the following day. While the work was continuing a huge explosion destroyed the aircraft and claimed the lives of several members of the salvage party plus two RAF airmen. It is assumed that the depth charges had blown up.
JIM CASTLES

Watchful... Under the watchful eyes of a 210 Squadron Catalina and an armed trawler, Sunderland G of the mainly Norwegian manned 330 Squadron awaits rescuers off the Faroes Islands. This was ML827 which was forced to ditch on May 12th 1945 - less than a week after the war in Europe had ended - following the failure of both starboard engines. After the crew was rescued by the trawler ML827 was left to sink the next day.
JOHN PEARCE

Two inches in it... There are just two recorded incidents in which a Sunderland actually landed on dry land - and in both cases it was a remarkable tale in which the crews survived.
For the crew of NJ186, of 423 Squadron, RCAF, Sunday May 20th 1945 is a date forever etched in the memory. Although peace had just been declared in Europe Sunderlands maintained their patrols for some time after VE-Day and F/Lt Gerry Allen and his crew - including a third pilot along for a familiarisation flight - were tasked with escorting an oil tanker and an anti-submarine patrol.
For their 700 hours start from RAF Castle Archdale, Northern Ireland, the weather was foul, and it did not improve as the heavily laden and armed Sunderland climbed slowly up through the murk. In cloud course was set for the patrol area and the radar brought into use as an aid to navigation. Less than an hour into the flight the pilots suddenly found themselves face-to-face with terra firma. The instant reaction of co-pilot F/Lt 'Ole' Olson in ramming the throttles forward and pulling back on the control column saved disaster, but the Sunderland 'touched bottom' on a rocky outcrop and lurched and slowed perceptibly. A grinding, crunching sound came at the same time - but the aircraft somehow stayed airborne.
It was later established that NJ186 had hit the highest point of the Mountains of Mourne in Ireland, some 12 miles off its intended track. Two inches higher and the Sunderland would have sauntered on undamaged; two inches lower and it would undoubtedly have crashed.
All the crew members were safe but wireless operator/air gunner, F/O Jim Miller, who was resting off duty on a bunk, had a particularly rude awakening. He came to covered in peat and debris - and straddling a ten foot gash in the hull. The adjoining bunk had disappeared - and so had Jim's hat, sucked into the void. As the Sunderland lurched around the sky crew colleagues managed to bring Jim into the upper part of the aircraft.
The crew's position was dire. They were still in cloud, the Sunderland was crippled and hard to control, the hull ruptured and - to add to their problems - it was discovered that the depth charges could not be ejected nor any fuel dumped due to damage sustained. The aircraft was carrying eight 250 lb depth charges and over 2000 gallons of petrol. With a hull ripped apart and one float missing there was no way this aircraft could land on water.
Miraculously the clouds parted allowing the pilots to bring the aircraft over the Irish Sea and the airfield at Jurby, on the Isle of Man, was spotted and headed for. Contact with the airfield's control tower certainly woke up the Sunday morning duty crew - a flying-boat was approaching and was going to land immediately!
In the extraordinary circumstances pilots Allen and Olson made a copybook landing on one of the concrete runways, the damaged hull screeching and scraping along the surface with bits of metal left in its wake. Finally, at 920 hours, what was left of NJ186 came to a halt. Amazingly all the crew were alive but co-pilot Olson had been seriously injured and was trapped in his seat. The crew was in further danger as fire broke out and the chances of the fuel tanks, ammunition and depth charges exploding was real. Olson was pulled from his seat and lowered to the ground and all the crew vacated the aircraft as quickly as they could - and not a moment too soon. The fuel tanks and the depth charges erupted, completely destroying the Sunderland. All that was left of the faithful NJ186 - which had valiantly stayed airborne and survived the crash landing - were two of the engines which were almost intact, a piece of the nose section and small pieces scattered everywhere over a devastated airfield. Windows were blown out in a three mile radius and the runway where the Sunderland had come to rest sported a 20 ft by 10 ft crater.
Olson and Miller - who had also been injured in the initial impact with the mountain - both recovered. Miller was also reunited with his officer's cap - recovered from the mountain - but the bunk and the galley which had also been sucked out were never found!
The all-Canadian crew of NJ186 on that fateful morning was: F/Lt Gerry Allen (pilot); F/Lt 'Ole' Olson (co-pilot); F/Lt A. D. C. 'George' Washington (observer); F/O Pat Doyle (WOp/AG); F/O Jim Miller (WOp/AG); P/O Scotty Robinson (WOp/AG); Sgt Harry Jepson (engineer); Sgt Len Clausen (engineer); Sgt Ralph Van Buskirk (gunner) and Sgt Jack Walker (gunner). The new pilot 'along for the ride' was Don Taylor.

** The only other occasion when a Sunderland was deliberately put down on land was on May 29th 1943 when F/O Gordon Singleton landed his damaged Mark II, T9114, on Angle Airfield, near Pembroke Dock. See Flying-Boat Queen Vol I and Gordon Singleton's own story, Singleton's War, for the full story of this historic landing).*

Photographs published in a Canadian magazine show NJ186 at its Castle Archdale mooring and Gerry Allen and his crew.
Via TERRY MacDONALD

Mystery... The identity of this almost completely submerged Mark V is not certain. One suggestion is that it may be VB885 which crashed off Calshot on February 13th 1946 with the loss of the ten crew. The official report stated that the aircraft - belonging to No 302 Ferry Training Unit - was attempting to regain the flare path in bad visibility when flying on three engines.
DOUG HOGGARTH via JOHN BRIGNELL

Chapter X Remembered

Training base... A Sunderlander's view of a station which played an important part in the lives of so many Sunderland crews - RAF Alness, on Scotland's Cromarty Firth. Originally known as Invergordon, this Scottish base took up the training mantle in June 1941 when No 4 (Coastal) Operational Training Unit moved in from Stranraer, with the officers' mess being established at nearby Dalmore House. Initially a variety of flying-boats - including elderly Stranraers, Singapores and Londons - operated from here before Sunderland completely took over. Here crews came together to learn about the aircraft before being posted to operational units. In February 1943 the station officially became known as RAF Alness and flying training continued until the summer of 1946 when 4 OTU transferred to Pembroke Dock.
The original of this photograph - dated 1943 - was found in recent years at Alness at the back of a desk. It is a rare view on part of a station which contributed much to the success story of the Sunderland and the many crews who flew and operated this remarkable aircraft.
ALISTAIR STIRRAT

Impressive... This most impressive memorial to Royal Air Force Alness (Invergordon) was unveiled in October 2001 by John Cruickshank, the Coastal Command VC and former Catalina pilot with No 210 Squadron.
ALNESS ASSOCIATION

Squadrons... Against the backdrop of superb views over the Sound of Kerrera, a memorial was dedicated in September 1998 to all who had served at RAF Oban, on Scotland's west coast. The memorial is located at Ganavan Sands, close to the town, where flying-boats were brought ashore for maintenance. Oban was home base to eight individual squadrons, operating Sunderlands, Catalinas, Stranraers, Lerwicks and examples of a very rare bird in RAF markings - the Martin Mariner. For two years No 302 Ferry Training Unit was also based here, latterly specialising in training Sunderland crews prior to long overseas flights.
ALISTAIR STIRRAT

Above right: The plaque which lists all the units which served at RAF Oban.
AUTHOR

Synonymous... Just across the Cattewater from the famous Hoe at Plymouth was RAF Mount Batten, long associated with flying-boats from its RNAS Cattewater days in World War One. In history it will ever be synonymous with two squadrons - No 204 RAF, which formed here in 1929 and ten years later took delivery of its first Sunderland, and No 10 Squadron, RAAF. No 204 departed in April 1940 and was replaced by the Australians who made Mount Batten their wartime home. Apart from a spell at Pembroke Dock in 1941 - following Luftwaffe raids in which a hangar and a Sunderland were wrecked - the Aussies flew from Plymouth for the rest of the war, writing a unique chapter into Coastal Command's story. Other flying-boat units used Mount Batten as a diversionary base as operational requirements - and the weather - often dictated. The photograph is a post-war view of the RAF Mount Batten peninsula which for many years was the main base for RAF marine craft.
ERIC MORTON

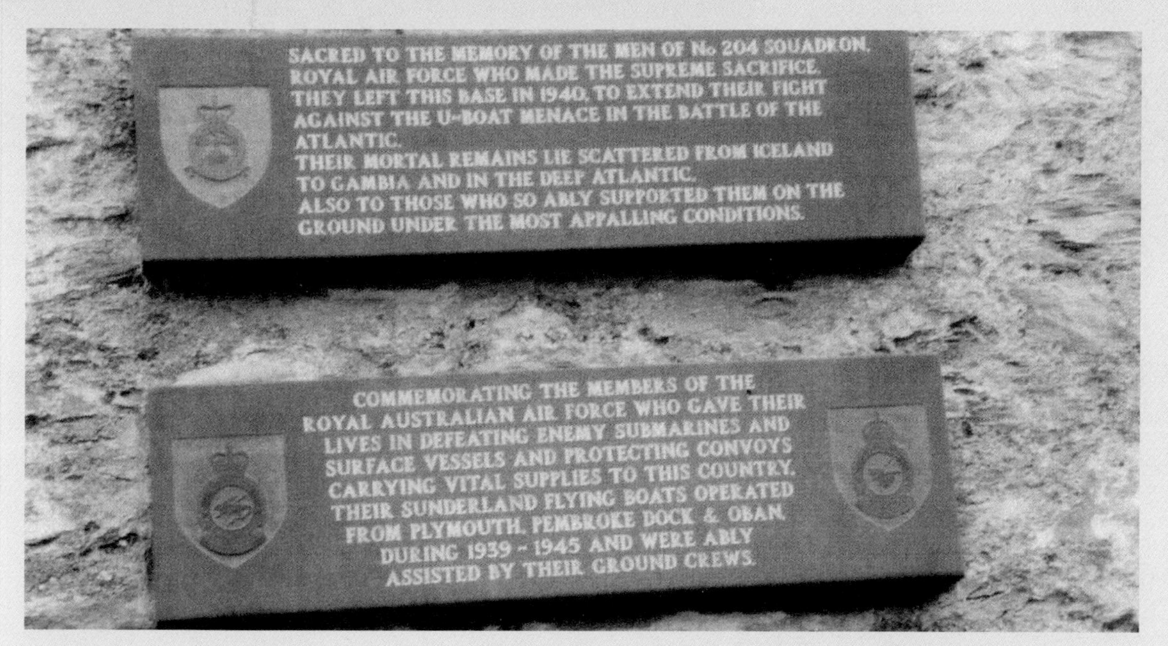

Plaques... A feature of the Mount Batten peninsula is the 'Tower', a circular fortification dating from Napoleonic times. In recent years two plaques have been unveiled here commemorating flying-boat units. One remembers No 204 Squadron and alongside the squadron crest is the wording: 'Sacred to the memory of the men of N0 204 Squadron, Royal Air Force, who made the supreme sacrifice. They left this base in 1940 to extend their fight against the U-Boat menace in the Battle of the Atlantic. Their mortal remains lie scattered from Iceland to Gambia and in the deep Atlantic. Also to those who so ably supported them on the ground under the most appalling conditions'.
The Australian connection with Nos 10 and 461 Squadrons is commemorated on the second plaque. The wording reads: 'Commemorating the members of the Royal Australian Air Force who gave their lives in defeating enemy submarines and surface vessels and protecting convoys carrying vital supplies to this country. Their Sunderland flying-boats operated from Plymouth, Pembroke Dock and Oban during 1939-1945 and we ably assisted by their ground crews'.
DARRELL JAGO

Reunions... Over a ten year period, from 1985 to 1995, Pembroke Dock relived its 'webfooter' days at five Flying-Boat Reunions, hosted by No 648 Branch of the Royal Air Forces Association. These were very special occasions for the community, rekindling memories of peacetime and wartime flying-boat days at PD, and were attended by 'webfooters' from all over the world. At the first reunion - in May 1985 - the chief guest was Air Vice-Marshal Donald Bennett, pioneer aviator and wartime leader of the Pathfinders bomber group. In 1932, as a young Pilot Officer, Donald Bennett had been stationed at Pembroke Dock and had learned his craft on flying-boats with the resident 210 Squadron. He unveiled a plaque - generously donated by Short Brothers, makers of the Sunderland and other famous flying-boats - which remembered all who served at RAF Pembroke Dock between 1930 and 1959 and commemorated those lost on operations. At subsequent reunions, plaques were also donated to the town by the Australians of Nos 10 and 461 Squadrons, the Canadians of No 422 Squadron and the Americans of Patrol Squadron 63 of the US Navy. And, at the final reunion in August 1995 - 50 years on from the end of the Second World War - a replica of the RAF Pembroke Dock Memorial Window was unveiled by John Cruickshank, VC. This remains on display in the town's library. Pembroke Dock's glory days of flying-boats are not forgotten.

Above: Air Vice-Marshal Bennett (left) is pictured unveiling the plaque, helped by Bill Millar, Chairman of No 648 Branch RAFA, and himself a 'webfooter' who joined 210 Squadron at PD in 1939.
MARTIN CAVANEY

The way it was...
A Sunderland on the slipway at Pembroke Dock, a familiar scene for two decades. This is ML745, a much travelled veteran which served in wartime with 228 Squadron and post-war did time with 209, 88 and 205 Squadrons. It joined 205/209 Squadron in early 1957 but was struck off charge within months of arriving at Seletar following an accident (see Chapter VI).
VIC BENSON

Chapter XI Squadron Badges

The majority of RAF and Commonwealth squadrons which operated Sunderlands had their own formally approved Badges. The RAF Badges are Crown Copyright/MoD.

10... The Atlantic and Australia are brought together in the Badge of 10 Squadron, Royal Australian Air Force. It depicts an Atlantic chimera pierced by an Australian aboriginal fishing spear. The simple motto - Strike first - speaks for itself.
LAWSWOOD COLLECTION

88... The Badge shows a serpent gliding and the French motto - 'En Garde' - means 'Be on your guard'. It is based on a World War I badge of Escadrille SPA 88 of the French Air Service which the squadron was associated with. No 88 was also know as the 'Hong Kong' squadron.
MRS DORIS McKAY

95... The Badge is described as 'On a mount of waves in the sea in front of a palm tree a crowned crane displayed'. It combines the large flying bird and palm, of West Africa, flying over the ocean. The motto has a similar theme - meaning 'I went out over the sea'.
WING COMMANDER STAN BAGGOTT COLLECTION

119... Another squadron adopting a strong maritime theme in its Badge, 119 has a sword, the point downwards, and an anchor in saltire. Round the clock operations are reflected in the motto, 'By night By day'.
LAWSWOOD COLLECTION

201... 'A seagull, wings elevated and addorsed' is how 201's badge is described. Apparently it was used unofficially long before formal approved by the College of Arms and the then King Edward VIII in May 1936 and was one of the first seven Badges awarded. The motto means 'Here and everywhere'.
TOM DEMPSTER JONES

202... As befitting a squadron so involved with the maritime tradition a familiar bird - a mallard alighting - was chosen for the official Badge approved in December 1937. The motto is a commanding 'Be always vigilant'.
ALAN SMITH

204... 'I seek my prey in the sea' is the motto of 204, the Badge featuring a cormorant perched in characteristic wing drying pose on a mooring buoy. The Badge is said to be based on a photograph taken by Aircraftsman Shaw, more famously known as Lawrence of Arabia.
RAF HERALDRY TRUST

205... The squadron's Malayan connections are reflected in the Badge and motto. The motto, in Malay, means 'First in Malaya', and the Badge is of a kris and a trident in saltire. The trident refers to its naval origins and the kris to its links with Malaya.
ALEC CARRIE

209... 'An eagle volant recursant descendant in pale, wings overture' is the official description. The eagle falling symbolises the destruction of famous World War I fighter ace Baron Manfred von Richthofen who may have fallen to the guns of the squadron, then operating fighters. The motto is 'Might and main'.
ALEC CARRIE

210... Often referred to as a dragon, the creature resplendent on 210's Badge is, in fact, a griffin. As befitting a squadron which reformed on flying-boats at Pembroke Dock in Wales, the motto is in Welsh and means 'Hovering in the Heavens'.
LAWSWOOD COLLECTION

228... A Latin phrase, chosen from a pocket dictionary, was adopted at the beginning of World War II as the motto for 228's Badge. It is variously translated as 'Help from the Heavens' or 'Help from the sky'. A winged helmet is the centrepiece.
F. STEELE

230... The Badge and motto link 230 with Malaya where it served on a number of occasions. 'In front of a palm tree eradicated, a tiger passant' is the official description and the motto - in Malay - means 'We seek far'.
PETER GRAY / D. RICHINGS

The RAF Heraldry Trust

Set up in 1996, the Trust continues to build up the definitive reference collection of heraldic history of the Royal Air Force. It is intended to paint every Badge granted to a unit of the RAF or the Commonwealth Air Forces.

Individuals, associations or organisations can commission the painting of a Badge and dedicate it as appropriate.

240... This squadron also chose a winged helmet; 240's version is silver with black wings. This is a Viking helmet, reflecting the squadron's time in Iceland and activity over Icelandic waters. The motto - also in Icelandic - means 'Guardian of the sea, guardian of the air'.
LAWSWOOD COLLECTION

330... Another Badge with a Viking theme, this was adopted by the Norwegian-manned squadron which operated Northrop floatplanes, Catalinas and Sunderlands in World War II. The Viking ship is in full sail before the sun and the Norwegian motto means 'Guarding the seas'.
RAF HERALDRY TRUST

422... A Shakespearean quotation - 'This arm shall do it' - was chosen by the mainly Canadian-manned 422 Squadron, the Badge showing 'A cubit arm holding in the hand a tomahawk'. The painted arm indicates that the native brave is at war.
SID BUTLER

423... A famous bird of the North Americas, the bald eagle, was adopted by another Royal Canadian Air Force unit, 423, for its Badge. With its talons outstretched it fully reflects the Latin motto which means 'We search and strike'.
JIM WRIGHT

461... 'They shall not pass unseen' is the splendid motto of the second Royal Australian Air Force squadron which operated Sunderlands in Coastal Command. The Badge is also apt for a submarine-hunting unit - showing 'a demi-shark couped, pierced by a harpoon'.
LAWSWOOD COLLECTION

490... A fearsome Maori weapon, a patu, gripped by a fist was chosen by the only Royal New Zealand Air Force squadron to operate Sunderlands in wartime. The motto means 'The Taniwha is in the air' - the Taniwha being a sea monster in Maori legend credited with supernatural powers.
ROYAL NEW ZEALAND AIR FORCE MUSEUM 990157

For further information please visit the website at ***www.rafht.org.uk*** or contact *The RAF Heraldry Trust, Chestnut Farm House, Ludford Road, Binbrook, Market Rasen, Lincolnshire, LN8 6DR* or e-mail ***Trust@RAFHT.org.uk***

Chapter XII Flying into the 1990s!

Realistic... Looking for all the world like the 'real thing', a one-tenth scale model of Sunderland III EK594 takes to the air over the Hinze Dam, Queensland, Australia. Made and flown by Geoff Reichelt, the model carries the marking RB-D of 10 Squadron, RAAF, which was Geoff's father's aircraft at Plymouth in wartime service. Geoff's set piece was to bomb a model U-Boat on the surface of the water, the whole scene being so realistic. This wonderful model was donated by Geoff to the present-day 10 Squadron and is displayed at the squadron's headquarters at RAAF Edinburgh, South Australia.
ANGUS McVINISH

On wheels!... In the early 1990s Dutch enthusiast Jan Hermkens built and flew a Mark II Sunderland - complete with beaching gear as undercarriage! It was a show stopper and prize winner at model events. The model also carried 10 Squadron markings, as RB-U, W3986. A photo of the actual aircraft appears in Chapter III.
Via WING COMMANDER VIC HODGKINSON